W9-ATT-075

PRAISE FOR *LIFE'S GREAT DARE*

You know that thing you've been wanting to do for a long time now, but you just keep putting off? Yes, that's the one. That thing that just popped into your mind—the conversation, the trip, the move, the job. We all have something, but there are obstacles, invisible or otherwise, getting in our way. In this book, Christa will dare you, with grace and firmness and wisdom, to be brave and finally do it. After all, what are you waiting for, anyway?

— **Allison Vesterfelt,** Author of *Packing Light*
allisonvesterfelt.com

When faced with pain, uncertainty or fear, we can become paralyzed, afraid to take the next step. But in this book, through her compelling reflections and moving personal story, Christa Hesselink points us to the real path toward the transformed life God calls us to: taking risks, moving forward, reaching out and opening up. Then we'll find freedom and the courage to persevere, no matter what life brings. So, don't play it safe. Follow Christa's example. Go. Jump. Dare!

— **Michael Messenger,** President, World Vision Canada
worldvision.ca

A helpful guide for anyone on the look out for the deeper waters of life. While we know that it may take a leap of faith, Christa reminds us that when in doubt, it's always better to jump afraid than to never jump at all.

— **Ali Raney,** The Lovelocks
thelovelocksband.com

The future belongs to those who have nothing to lose. This is truth Christa Hesselink captures in this wonderfully written and personal book, *Life's Great Dare*. Each page points toward the possibility of a life lived vulnerably, passionately and deeply with God. Christa's personal journey is the mirror held up for all of us to see how life might be more adventure and less antiseptic. If you have ever wanted to live the faithful life with abandon, this is the book to read!

— **Gary V. Nelson,** Author of *Leading in DisOrienting Times*,
President, Tyndale University College and Seminary

Some mountains are virtually impossible to climb without a trusted guide. Inner personal transformation is one of these mountains. Christa is one of these guides. Her compelling story, seasoned wisdom, and artful style will turn what may at first feel like a daunting task into a truly inspiring journey. I invite you to take "life's great dare", open your heart and join her on this upward path. The view that lies ahead is incredible!

— **Tim Day,** Author of *God Enters Stage Left*
timday.org

Christa has the wonderful ability to encourage and convict us in the same sentence. She beautifully uses biblical texts and personal stories, convincing us to submit and be transformed by a loving God and to take part in what she calls the ultimate double-dare. Whether bungee jumping in South Africa or walking the El Camino, her life is a true testament of what it means to follow Jesus wholeheartedly and with great conviction.

— **Melinda Estabrooks,** International Speaker, TV & Radio Host
melindaestabrooks.com

Life's Great Dare unveils how God is willing to change us when we are willing to let him. Christa weaves her own powerful story of ongoing transformation together with immensely practical ways of finding radical freedom through risking our lives to God!

— **Bruxy Cavey,** Teaching Pastor of The Meeting House
and Author of best-seller *The End of Religion*
bruxy.com

Jump in! *Life's Great Dare* is a challenge to embrace a fully engaged life. Christa is a persuasive friend along the journey, inviting us to live an abundant life. My hope is people far and wide are impacted by the message of this book!

— **Rich Birch**
UnSeminary.com

Life's Great Dare is for anyone who has a little voice inside asking them to live a bigger, bolder, more adventurous life. Through story-telling and inspired words, this book equips you to pursue a path of personal transformation, and leaves you wanting to say YES to life's great dare (and maybe even a few double-dares)!

— **Zoë Neuman,** The Lovelocks
thelovelocksband.com

Life's Great Dare will take you on a transformational journey! If you're simply looking for information, this isn't your book. But if you desire to experience freedom in encountering God's love and following Jesus, you will want to read, and soak, in these compelling truths.

— **Dr. Craig Sider,** President, New York City Leadership Center
nycleadership.com

Christa's reflections on God's movement in her life help us recognize God's movement in ours. Pondering challenges, perplexities, and losses that she's experienced, she invites us all to be more fully embraced by God's love. Her blend of wit and wisdom, honesty and hopefulness, not to mention her wonderful way with words, will hearten you as it did me.

— **Arthur Boers,** Author of *The Way is Made by Walking: A Pilgrimage Along the Camino de Santiago* and *Living into Focus: Choosing What Matters in an Age of Distraction* *arthurboers.com*

Christa has given us a deeply personal and gut-twistingly vulnerable work... in her words a "self-hope, not a self-help book". And yet as she shows us over and over, it is not about the self at all. She takes us to the culturally unpopular places of sacrifice, suffering and surrender. Rich with stories from childhood, from the Gospel, and from last week, Christa reminds us powerfully of the joy available when we live with hands open and upturned, "ready to receive instead of living life with fists tightly clenched around things that give me the illusion of control".

— **Rick Cober Baumen,** Executive Director, Mennonite Central Committee Ontario *mcco.ca*

READER REVIEWS

Life's Great Dare leaves you energized, inspired, and prepared to fling open a door towards an abundant life. It's the kind of book you read, then give to a friend to read, but then they go get their own copy because you've highlighted and cried all over yours.

— Natalie

With such a friendly and unassuming manner, Christa's depth of life experience nearly catches you off guard. Christa owns her story and teaches us how to do the same. Readers can be thankful that she has paused long enough on her own pilgrimage to share some of the beauty of the transformation God has produced in her life so far.

— Jared

This book is like a conversation over tea with Christa. She shares remarkable stories, challenges you to consider your own stories, and then encourages you to be brave and live the life God calls you to live.

— Lindsay

You can't make it through this book without being both moved and changed. In it, Christa dares us to take a risk... to say yes, to give up, to step out, to receive and to grow closer to the God who loves us unimaginably. I'm already recommending it to others and can't wait to see stories shaped through the vulnerability and challenge found in these pages.

— Sarah

In *Life's Great Dare*, Christa takes you on her journey of being intentional about pursuing more love, peace, and joy. I was challenged to make the space to be transformed. The book dared me to have a fresh perspective to the everyday reality of my life.

— *Cathy*

Christa's *Life's Great Dare* is an extraordinarily honest, moving, sometimes painfully heartbreaking and ultimately uplifting account of one remarkable woman's journey of surrender and transformation. Through Christa's life story, she details the process of transformation, partnering with God, her rebirth, being re-made into a better version of herself, and her journey closer to that abundant life we all crave. And the most beautiful aspect of Christa's book is that we can all follow her lead and do the same...if we take up life's great dare.

— *Patrick*

ISBN 978-0-9949172-0-1

Copyright © 2016 Christa Hesselink. All rights reserved.

No part of this book may be reproduced or transmitted in any form or by any means, electronic or mechanical including photocopying, recording or by any information storage and retrieval system, without written permission from Christa Hesselink. The only exception is in the case of brief quotations embodied in critical articles or reviews.

Exterior Design: Dave Fretz
Interior Design: Diego Lopez
Cover Photo Credit: Luke Pamer and Dominik Schröder

LIFE'S GREAT DARE

Risking It All for the Abundant Life

christa hesselink

For Mom and Dad who dare to live courageously.
And for Todd—so dearly missed and never forgotten.

CONTENTS

INTRODUCTION: THE DARE

"To dare is to lose one's footing momentarily.
Not to dare is to lose oneself."
— Søren Kierkegaard

I always picked the dare. Every time.

When I was a kid, I played a game with my friends called Truth, Dare, Double-Dare, Promise to Repeat. We played it in all sorts of places: the back corner of the yard when we were bored of tag or hide-and-seek, or in the wee morning hours of a slumber party when we were getting tired and silly. It was a simple game, really. Whoever's turn it was had to choose one of the four options, while the other kids decided what the person had to do. I loved the game because it always made me feel nervous and excited like something extraordinary was going to happen. But I hated it too because it always felt like it had the potential to steal away a bit of my dignity. It felt risky.

Choosing Truth meant you'd have to answer any question that was asked of you. "Do you like Tim?" or "Have you ever kissed someone?" (You know, the earth-shattering questions ten-year-olds ask!) You never knew what was going to be asked of you but you had to answer.

To pick Dare generally entailed doing something ridiculous or disgusting. I remember eating a hot dog topped with ice cream, broccoli and soy sauce. I was also dared to run around the outside of the house in the pouring rain, screaming, "I'm going crazy!"

With Double-Dare, the stakes got really high. Any takers had to do something absolutely outrageous, the mortifyingly unthinkable. Call up a boy and tell him you liked him or confess to your mom about something bad you had done.

Promise to Repeat always seemed the most benign to me. To choose this one usually meant an embarrassing admission of something silly: "I like to pick my nose and eat it" or "I love ketchup in my chicken noodle soup." It wasn't the stuff to rock the earth's foundations.

I always picked the dare.

It wasn't because I had some secret truth I didn't want to share, or was too embarrassed to say something silly. I just liked getting off my chair and doing something. I liked the action and adventure of it all. It was simultaneously exhilarating and terrifying, and I always felt better after I was finished. The pay-off in accepting the dare seemed worth the struggle.

Nothing has changed for me as an adult either: I still pick the dare—at least I try to. A dare shows me what I'm made of. It gives me a glimpse of the things that scare me, and the grit I've got to try anyway. Accepting a dare always moves my story forward. It changes things.

I dare you to sign up for that course.

I dare you to ask him out.

I dare you to be honest with how you feel.

I dare you to take that trip.

I dare you to give it one more try.

But what about the double-dare? I never picked Double-Dare and neither did my friends. It was just way too scary. Does anyone ever pick a true double-dare in life? Risk it all? Take a gamble on something that feels audacious? Do we hazard our own comfort for something more exhilarating?

I've had big stuff happen in my life, stuff that left me feeling more vulnerable than any game ever could. I've also had little things throw me off, things that shouldn't make me feel insecure and vulnerable but that do. But to choose that kind of dare—the double-dare? What would it take to accept the sort of dare that feels like our sense of security is on the line? Can I even imagine stepping into that sort of vulnerability by choice?

What could possibly feel important enough to accept the dare to risk it all?

This is a story of the one thing worth risking it all for. This is my story of surrender and what happens when I accept life's great dare. Your story might not be as dramatic as mine has been at times—or as mundane as it has been at others—but I've come to see that life's great dare is offered to every one of us.

Accepting the greatest dare is worth it.

EMBRACING THE DARE

Dare: to have the boldness to try; venture; hazard;
to meet defiantly; face courageously

1

The Haircut That Changed My Life

"...and then the day came
when the risk to remain tight in a bud
was more painful than the risk it took to blossom."
— Anaïs Nin

When I was ten years old, I was enamored with Little Orphan Annie. You know, the little girl with a big smile, freckles, and a hairdo of short, tight, red curls. I loved her hair. I had limp, bone-straight, brown hair—the kind that couldn't hold a curl if its life depended on it. Even my mom never knew what to do with my hair. Barrettes and bows would slip right out. So, with the wisdom I had acquired in a decade of life, I decided to get my first curly perm just before the start of summer vacation.

I should have guessed that there was something unnatural about the whole thing when I smelled the combination of burning hair and toxic chemicals. Instead, all fear was replaced by utter fascination when I found out that I would not need to brush my hair anymore—instead, I'd get to use a new steel pick comb to "poof my 'fro". When I see pictures now, I laugh at how ridiculous I looked. But I remember having the time of my life that summer. Everything was just more fun with tight, short curls!

Have you ever noticed how a haircut can change the way you deal with life? For good or bad (and sometimes very, very bad), I've always felt different after leaving a hair appointment. Sometimes the feeling lasts only an hour, while other times it lasts until I wash the stylist's magic from my locks, but I've never stepped out of the chair feeling exactly the same way I did when I went in. I'm always transformed.

When I was in college, I got one of the worst haircuts ever! I was broke and the cheapest place to get a haircut in town was offering a deal. Can someone say "red flag"? I have two distinct memories of that afternoon. I remember feeling terrified when the young stylist started cutting my hair with the same amateurish approach I used when I was eight and took the scissors to my Barbie's hair. My second memory is of walking back to the campus along a busy highway, crying in the pouring rain. I was soaked and felt like a drowned rat. What was worse was that I looked like one too, even once my hair dried. My haircut was terrible: uneven, limp and completely out of style.

There was one haircut, however, that changed my life forever.

I had just quit my full-time job and didn't have another one lined up. I was planning on spending the summer finishing up my graduate thesis and taking stock of my life. I spent much of my newfound freedom (a better term than unemployment, no?) traveling around visiting friends. One such trip brought me to Chicago in May to visit my good friend Jill.

Jill and I are a lot alike but it would be fair to say that she is much more spontaneous than I am. I have never been accused of being impulsive—ever. I love surprises and spur-of-the-moment fun, but I also really enjoy planning and thinking things through.

One day, Jill and I were musing over the fact that we had known each other for over a decade and would soon be turning thirty. I told her how I was excited to finish my studies later that summer, and that my plan was to find a new job and then get a cool new haircut later in the fall.

She stared at me blankly, like I was speaking a different language. Her mouth curled with confusion. "Why would you wait five whole months to get a cool new haircut? Why wouldn't you do it now?"

It wasn't like I didn't have the money for it. And I already planned how I wanted to get it cut. For some reason, though, getting a new style didn't fit into my calculated master plan until later. I explained I wanted to wait. She gave me a similar look, but this time with a hint of frustration.

Then she pleaded, "Christa, would you just do one spontaneous thing in your life!"

I was shocked. Was she mad at me? Was I being ridiculous? Was that a challenge? Did she not think I could call up a place and get my hair cut that day—right there on the spot? She was daring me to make a change.

Before I knew it, the words were rolling out of my mouth. "Fine. Call someone. I'll get my hair cut today!"

That afternoon, I hesitantly followed Jill into a trendy, downtown Chicago salon. I walked up the stairs to the cool loft studio all the while second-guessing this newfound spontaneity.

"What am I doing?" I thought to myself. "I'm not even going to a stylist that I know. No one I know has ever gone here before. Isn't this place a bit too cool for me? I better not walk out of here with blue hair!"

I rounded the corner and a petite man with bright blue (!) hair of all different lengths greeted me with a thick Venezuelan accent. "Hello, my name is Angel and I'll be cutting your hair today."

Oh. My. Word. What had I done?

As I sat in the chair, I quickly began thinking how best to describe the type of hairstyle I wanted without offending him. How do you tell a scissor-happy guy with blue hair you're just not that cool and that your goal is to be able to walk out of his salon without wearing a bag over your head?

"Well, Angel," I explained, "I'm not from around here. In fact, I... ah...I don't even live in a big city like Chicago. Actually, I'm from a smaller town...in Canada...a lot smaller, really. I mean I'm young, and want to look good, but I'm just not that edgy—you get me?"

Honestly, I'm not sure what Angel thought. He must have smelled the fear and pathetic all over me because he assured me many times he knew what he was doing. Finally, before I submitted myself completely to the hands of this artist, I explained one last time, "Angel, I'm looking for Canadian-farm-girl-funky. Can you do that?"

With a smirk and a nod he started to cut.

Needless to say, the haircut was one of the best I've ever had.

The cut framed my face and made my eyes pop. The highlights looked perfect. I hopped off his chair feeling free, and looking cuter than Orphan Annie. Not only was my haircut new and fresh, but so was the bounce in my step as Jill and I walked out of the salon.

Love Big and Bold

Countless times since that warm May day, I have heard Jill's voice in my head, "Christa, would you just do one spontaneous thing in your life?" As a result, I've done things I hadn't dreamed of doing—taking trips, speaking my mind, trying new things. It really was the haircut that changed my life!

But in recent years, it hasn't been Jill's voice that I've been hearing. Perhaps it never was at all. No, the quiet voice daring me out of my comfort zone towards something new is that of someone with far more influence. Someone who knows me much better than even Jill ever could. It is the gentle voice of God asking me to be open—open to being transformed. It's as if he knows there is a better version of my life waiting to be uncovered, a life with more love and less pain, more joy and less fear, more peace and less anxiety.

If you're like me, you crave that kind of life. You want a life that feels more like an adventure than a job. You sense there is a better version of yourself out there and you want to go after it. You're tired of feeling the burden of "trying to be better" and yet you don't want to give up. You've been living a stale, monochromatic life but you're craving the technicolor promises of an abundant life.

I think most of us sense there is something better, deeper and more meaningful in life. Something good and true and honest to hold onto. Aren't we all after a little more love? Don't we all want more peace, more joy? I know I do. I look for those things around every corner and under all the stones. I want a life of purpose and peace. I'm always searching for a big, bold love that will make my heart secure. I want a full, beautiful, and abundant life.

So I asked God to point me in that very direction. And he did. He pointed me in exactly that direction. "You want a big, bold, abundantly full life, Christa? Perfect. Let me transform you. Transformation is the pathway to the treasure you are searching for."

I had always seen the process of personal life change as a difficult activity that only mature, conscientious people strived for—some self-help program that was good for me, like vitamins or flossing, an obligation in personal discipline in order to be in God's good books. I thought that maybe God begrudged the business of transformation—that he had to fix me up so he could love me more.

But I started to wonder if I had it all wrong.

What if transformation wasn't about God making me more perfect so he could love me more, but instead was about changing me so I could experience his love more perfectly? Seeing personal life change as the way to find a treasure God wants to give me? Well, that would be a whole different story. That would feel like pure gift and I would want to get my hands on as much of it as possible. Transformation would be something I could actually look forward to and embrace.

Maybe, like me, you're tired of the self-help approach and know you don't have what it takes to solve your own issues. You're desperate for another way out. You want to experience love in bigger and bolder ways and you wonder if God has anything to do with it. You hear the promises that life could be full of peace and joy now—and yet you're not sure how to go after it. Or maybe you've always known God is in the business of making us better versions of ourselves but you're not really sure how it all works. At the end of the day, you know there is more and you're not willing to settle, but you just aren't sure what your next step is.

That's why I wrote this book.

None of us lives the Pinterest-perfect life that we crave, the life where everything is just right and we feel completely satisfied and secure. I don't know about you, but sometimes I feel like crumbling under all the brokenness and pain I see and feel. Sickness, abuse, war, poverty, greed, loneliness and despair. We don't have to look very far to see the fractured, empty places in us and in our world that need an infusion of love, joy and peace.

Brokenness takes all shapes and sizes too. Tragedy strikes and we struggle to move forward in healthy ways. We can feel buried in guilt and regret. We have everything we need, yet we still feel unhappy and lonely. We have places of fear and sadness we're afraid to address and we continue to carry wounds and hurt from when we were kids. We tend to operate out of fear and anxiety or a heavy weariness instead of hopeful optimism towards life. We're restless and unsettled people.

We've all got our own version of brokenness and we all want to fall in love with life again.

Finding the Treasure

Craving to live with more love and less fear is normal. We all want more freedom and peace, less anxiety and loneliness. We are naturally on a mission for more justice and generosity. I recognize this deep-seated inclination when I check out the news headlines. My heart sinks at stories of pain, and sings when someone is triumphant and has overcome the odds. You and I know when we see a truly selfless act of kindness. We respond to beauty and repel what isn't. Our dreams for our world and ourselves are filled with more freedom and fullness, purpose and light. Each of us wants to live an abundant and satisfying life.

There's a story Jesus told his friends to illustrate the value of abundant life. In this story, he calls this way of life a treasure because it's a life filled with love and generosity, freedom and peace, justice and purpose. It's a flourishing Kingdom of beauty and truth.

"The Kingdom of Heaven is like a treasure that a man discovered hidden in a field. In his excitement, he hid it again and sold everything he owned to get enough money to buy the field. Again, the Kingdom of Heaven is like a merchant on the lookout for choice pearls. When he discovered a pearl of great value, he sold everything he owned and bought it!" (Matthew 13:44-46)

We can learn a lot from this very short story. First of all it's clear there is, in fact, a treasure to be found. It is very real, and it's priceless. There's no dispute that the treasure is worth everything. Jesus gives the impression there is a "we're-much-better-off-with-it" quality to the treasure even though it costs a lot. It's clear it is not something we naturally have in our possession—we have to go out and find it. It's rare, hidden and not entirely obvious or typical. The treasure we are after is not like stones lying on the surface of a field, easily seen by any passerby. We have to dig for this treasure. But it's worth it because it's special and it is ours for the taking. Sound too good to be true? Of course it does. Jesus makes it clear this treasure is pure gift from God.

Even though it seems there is no regret in going after the treasure, obtaining it comes at a cost. It appears that the only thing we're responsible for is to look for the treasure. Seek it and make it our own. But we can't take the path of least resistance. We must let go of the things we value most in order to get it. We must step into vulnerability and sacrifice what brings us comfort now for something better.

Imagine what the man who sold everything felt like—especially before he purchased that field. The time between emptying his hands of all his earthly possessions and going back to that field to dig up the treasure. What if someone had stumbled on the treasure and purchased the field before him? What if the price of the field went up, costing more than he thought, or more than he had to buy it?

Think about the pearl merchant: might he have doubted the flawless pearl was as valuable as the belongings he just sold? Going after the treasure feels risky because we lose some of our control. Yet, just as the story tells us, we can go after the treasure with joy and excitement because we know it is exactly what our hearts crave. When we hold the treasure in our hands, we'll be truly free.

Jesus doesn't leave us wondering whether the gamble paid off. The field and pearl were bought. There's no hint of regret. The trade-off for the treasure was worth it and both men are clearly much better off. The more we learn about this Kingdom of God and the abundant life, the more we realize that it's worth the sacrifice, because the treasure always leads to the deepest kind of freedom we crave.

Don't get me wrong: going after this treasure has all the makings of a double-dare. Pursuing a full, abundant life feels incredibly risky. Being open to transformation is an invitation for someone else to take the lead, and for us to give up the lives we know for something new.

But here's what I'm learning: when that small, tender voice stirs within me, it's calling me on an adventure. I'm being invited to be vulnerable and surrender to a plan that is far greater than one I could ever create for myself. I'm being asked to let go of my control, and trust that I'll be okay, even if I don't know how it will all turn out. Surrendering to transformation requires I open up my hands with palms ready to receive instead of living life with fists tightly clenched around things that give me the illusion I have control.

Jesus speaks softly and gently. He asks me to loosen my grasp on the things I think will bring me life. He never forces open my tight grip but waits for me to unfurl my fingers and expose the soft, most vulnerable parts of my life to him. It's here he places a gift: his own strong hand that leads me to this life of freedom and love that I crave.

I'm invited to forgive a friend instead of holding on to the hurt. I'm prompted to let go of my tight grip on worrying about my image and trust that I'm lovely just the way I am. Jesus asks me to be generous with my time and money, knowing it will truly make me free. The treasure is buried deep and the excavation to find it happens in my own heart.

I want to be just like those two people from Jesus' story who sold everything. I want to risk it all and go after the treasure. I want to hold it in my hand. Don't you?

Why All the God Stuff?

Let me just pause here and speak to those of you who may like the sound of significant life change but you're not really sure about all this God stuff. Truth is, you may not even be comfortable with the label "God". Perhaps you are more comfortable with a different name such as "The Divine" or "Love". Whatever you choose to call this "Higher Power", I hope you don't get tripped up in the language that I'm using throughout the book.

In moments like these, I wish we could sit in comfy chairs, face to face, over a glass of wine or a cup of coffee to talk it over. I think the question about where God fits into this deserves some real attention. Even if you're not sure what you believe or where you stand on all this God talk, I'm asking that you give it three more minutes as you read and consider this next idea.

This conversation about transformation and an abundant life is pretty macro, wouldn't you say? It's about the big, important things in life. I wonder if you're reading this book because you're at a point where you're trying to put some of the puzzle pieces of life together but you're not sure what picture you are trying to make. It's impossible to know how the pieces fit together if you don't have a vision of what it's supposed to look like. I believe God's vision for the picture of your life is the best one, and he knows how all the pieces are to fit together.

There have been many people who have come before you with the same inkling there is something more to this life but not very confident on where to land. That's okay. I love how Dag Hammarskjöld, former UN Secretary-General and Nobel Prize winner describes it, "I don't Who—or What—put the question, I don't know when it was put. I don't even remember answering. But at some moment I did answer 'yes' to Someone—or Something—and from that hour I was certain that existence is meaningful and that, therefore, my life, in self-surrender, had a goal."

Indulge me for a few more moments. The Bible tells us that God, the creator and source of all things, humbled himself and came to earth in the form of his son Jesus. I know it's a mind bender if you've never really thought about it before. And let's be honest, some of you went to church as kids, and the very thought of the God of the Bible makes you cringe or leaves you confused. But I would bet the farm that as you get to know the real Jesus (perhaps for the very first time), you'll see the best picture of Divine Love who is pursuing you; a God who comes to you with a wild love; a God who knows you better than you know yourself and wants to guide you. Jesus is known as a rescuer and his way of saving us is profound.

God promises to meet us in our loss and longings if we ask him too. He doesn't look at us as an outsider would, cringing at the sight of our deep hurts. No, he is well acquainted with what is on my list of longings. He understands the ways I feel hurt and tired. He knows my sharp edges, underdeveloped boundaries and immature habits. Instead of staring in disgust or gazing in embarrassment at those places that need repair, he enters into my life knowingly, carefully, lovingly.

Sound too good to be true? Too difficult to believe? The truth is, I need a God who is too good to be true. Don't you? I need to follow a God who shakes the foundations of what's believable—a God who is mysterious and powerful and calls himself Love. When you've heard my whole story, you'll know how much I've needed a God who is God-sized. Otherwise, why bother?

This book is about helping all of us understand a bit more about personal transformation and how to take some concrete and personal next steps. Having this "Someone—or Something" intimately part of your life is hands down the most important part of personal life change. I think you've discovered without this, it is impossible to find the treasure you're truly seeking.

Thank you for considering the real Jesus in all of this. If you feel like you need to know more or just want to chat about this stuff, find someone who you can see follows Jesus. Ask questions. You won't get all the answers, but hopefully you'll get some guidance on how to get started. I know you won't regret it. Inviting God into your journey is the best thing you'll ever do. And just like every transformation, it starts with being open and surrendering to something bigger than us. It starts with being open to Love.

For those of us who are already following Jesus, our relationship with him requires daily attention. If we go back to that puzzle analogy, let's not forget we're doing this puzzle with God, not on our own. Pastor John Ortberg reminds us that "we do not just drift into becoming the best version of ourselves." Becoming the best version of ourselves is not a solitary journey either. If you've been out of the practice of spending some daily time with Jesus, perhaps this is the best place for you to start. Get down on the floor with him, puzzle pieces spread out, and follow his lead. Those of us who follow Jesus have hope in this process. We don't just submit to life, and somehow become transformed, hoping it all turns out okay in the end. We are invited to submit to the One who created us because he loved us. We have Someone who is transforming us from the inside out.

I once heard someone say she was attracted to the idea of being daring, not because she was particularly good at it but because she wanted to be. I love that. Regardless of how you're feeling right now, either full of courage or shirking in the shadows, we all want to be the type of people to embrace a dare.

So let's give it a shot. Let's say "yes".

Because "yes" really does change everything.

YES CHANGES EVERYTHING

*"How glorious the splendor of a human heart
that trusts that it is loved."*
— *Brennan Manning*

I've never ever had trouble believing that God is creative or powerful or good.

As a child, my sense of awe for sunsets and stars was big and it hasn't waned as I've gotten older. Harvest moons and the sound of the ocean always feel like signs of God on display. Knowing God is big and good? No, that's not where my trouble lies. Calling God Creator and Sustainer, Defender and Provider has always seemed appropriate, and using words like powerful and creative fit well too. I've never struggled to believe God has the power to shake the world or the creativity to captivate my gaze—my trouble has always been to feel his love.

Understanding that God is powerful is not the same as *feeling* his love.

Believing God is creative is not the same as *feeling* his love.

Knowing God is good is not the same as *feeling* his love.

Feeling makes all the difference.

A couple of years ago I realized I had two questions I needed to get answers for. Just two. But they were the big ones—the kind of questions that could tumble and crumble it all. Asking them felt like going somewhere where oxygen might disappear—daring the essence that sustained me to vanish. But I knew it was time to ask them because the questions were burning black right through me. Burning me out.

"God, do you really love me just the way I am?"

"Can I have a full life of love and joy now?"

I had gotten stuck. Real stuck. These weren't casual, fleeting questions. These were the heart-stopping, curl-up-under-the-covers sorts of thoughts that were threatening to undo me. I could no longer drown out the slippery and convincing voice urging me to go deep into the pit. I'd been living a long while wondering if I'd have to swallow down a hard "no" to these questions.

"No, you are not loved just the way you are. You are a mess."

"No, an abundant life here and now is just an illusion—there's too much pain for joy."

On my search for this abundant life we've been talking about, I kind of hoped I could skip over these gnawing questions and get on with living. It was like one of those awkward phases of puberty you want to avoid. I was hoping that somehow I could magically be transformed even if I didn't get the answers I was longing for. But, if what

I truly wanted was an abundant and full life, I had an inkling I would need to first discover and feel just how much God loved me.

Intuitively, I knew that it would make all the difference if I could receive a confident "yes" to those two questions. I knew that feeling God's love had the power to change everything. Imagine if I could say:

"Yes, God loves me. Sure, I'm a mess, but I'm secure. I am enough just the way I am."

"Yes, joy is for now. Peace is for now. An abundantly full life is for now!"

Yes. Changes. Everything.

I never expected that my quest towards finding this treasure of an abundant life would force me back to square one. To Love. God's love.

Life is Beautiful

What do the pathway of personal transformation and the love of God have to do with each another anyway?

It's an interesting question, really. Why is God so interested in transforming me in the first place? Does he need to make me better so he can love me more? Am I not enough just the way I am? Will he love me more if those broken parts in me are made new?

For the longest time I was absolutely sure that the reason God transforms us was because he needed to clean us up for his sake. As if the ultimate goal was for me to be perfect like Jesus so God could love me like he loved his own Son. Without me being cleaned up, it would be impossible for God to love me—I was just too messed up.

It's no wonder I have struggled for so long to feel God's love: knowing I'm not perfect meant I always felt so aware of my inability to be good enough. Deep down I knew that the equation (I need to change in order to be loved more) couldn't be true, but something always seemed to block me from really trusting my instincts.

Asking these questions is probably as old as time itself. It seems like the human mission, at its very core, is about the search for security, intimacy and wholeness. Who hasn't wondered whether or not they are truly loved just the way they are? Haven't we all asked ourselves if there's a type of love out there that would make us feel completely safe? Isn't the human quest to discover just how high the ceiling is on love and joy?

Isn't our life's expedition about the search for the "yes"?

Yes, you are loved and enough.

Yes, love is yours for the taking.

Yes, life is beautiful.

It was the same thing in the Garden. You know the story—Adam and Eve, the serpent and God. When contemplating eating from the forbidden, the first ones were asking the same questions that I am—that you are. Where can I find the fullness of love and security? Can I find what I'm looking for with God? Am I better on my own? Rather than remaining secure and fulfilled in God's love and acceptance, they considered that their own ways might lead to greater abundance and fulfillment. They decided to eat from the tree of "I know what's best".

I understand what Adam and Eve were up to. Just like you and me, they were hard-wired for intimacy and love. Their DNA sang of the need for connection and belonging with each other and with their Creator. They were designed for the fullness of life. Like me, they wondered whether their deepest longings were being met. They wondered—like I do—how to have the fullest life of peace, joy and love. That's why they took matters into their own hands.

They were free to love God (or not), which meant they were free to wonder whether God was able to give them the love they longed for. Their wondering led to their wandering, and their wandering led to them wanting more.

Henri Nouwen, an incredibly wise priest and scholar, once said, "Ever since the snake said, 'The day you eat of this tree your eyes will be open and you will be like gods, knowing good from evil' (Genesis 3:5) we have been tempted to replace love with power." I'm just like Adam and Eve. I've wandered out of trusting God's love was enough to secure me, and into wanting the power to control it for myself.

I understand the math full well and the equation is always the same: when I trust that I am loved, I know I am enough. When I know I am enough, I feel secure. When I feel secure, I am able to give and receive more love. It's a beautiful cycle. Peace begets more peace, joy begets more joy and love begets more love. And the fullness of love is the fullness of life.

Believe it or not, the big story of the Bible is about God pursuing his creation with relentless love. God's method is not to retaliate—it's to rescue. God isn't the big bad guy in the sky just waiting to pounce on us for all the crap we pull. He isn't scouring the land to point a finger at our mistakes. Is this something that surprises you? It kind of took me by surprise. I always thought God was in the business of fixing me because I wasn't perfect enough for him. I thought he was dutifully working to mend me, to make me more respectable so he could stand being in the same room as me. Maybe I had got it wrong. Perhaps God's motivation to repair me is to make me able to know and experience more of his love. What about you? Why do you think God wants you to become the best version of yourself?

In our cheaply made, throw-it-away culture, we may have a hard time wrapping our minds around this, but God doesn't assess our inherent worth based on our perfection (or lack of it). He finds us completely worthy just because we are, because he made us. He doesn't love us any less because we're broken. In fact, the care and time he takes to restore our lives is just another way he shows how much he loves us—when you create something out of deep love, you make it your business to do whatever you can to fix it when it breaks. He wants us to flourish for our sake. He wants us to experience the very best. His desire is for us to have more of what is most important—more peace, more joy, more love. God has gone (and still goes) to great lengths to repair us because he wants us to experience this abundant life. As the infectiously loveable author Bob Goff put it, it's what "Love Does". God loves us. It's what he does. That's the reason why transformation happens.

When we stop to think about what God is really up to in this world, we can get a sense of how his heart beats for us. He has committed himself to one grand plan: to conquer the dark and flood it with his light and radiance and love. His mission is a wild and loving pursuit. What does this mean for you and me? It means God won't rest until we've been completely made new. It means that he will be relentless in redeeming every part of our lives so that we will be made truly free. Our fears and anxieties, jealous tendencies and the source of our sadness, our pettiness and pain—they will all be uncovered, excavated and healed. God's endgame is for you and me to be perfectly free: completely and utterly able to live in the most intimate, unencumbered union with him. The starting point of the transformed life is God's deep love for us. The destination is the same—more love for us, for others and for God.

Drenched in Love

Still, I can remember many days when I wished someone would say or do something to help me feel more loved by God. I hoped that by some miraculous turn of events while I slept, I'd wake up in the morning and suddenly feel God's love in my heart instead of just knowing it in my head. I would read books, have hard conversations and try to journal my way out of the corner—all the while wondering why I couldn't feel God's love.

The truth is, I don't think anyone can say anything to make you feel more loved by God. Feeling something isn't like taking in information that is absorbed once it's been clearly communicated.

I can tell you, though, that when I started to grasp how God sees me in my brokenness and fragility, I opened up to see and feel his love in new ways.

Recently, I've begun to take God at his word when he describes himself as love. I've started to realize: What if God is showing me how much he loves me through every created thing? What if God creates and sustains all of creation, not only to show his power, but also to show you and me his love? The grapefruit and gravity, taste buds and the tadpole—everything exists because of love. Eyeballs and irises, music and marshmallows—every single thing is a gift saturated in God's love for you and me because the very essence of God is love.

What if we looked up at the skies and recognized God's pulsing love in every star? Could cloudless, star-studded nights be more about God showing us how much he loves us than a display of his awesome power? Or what about the intricate and fanciful design of a flower? Could the patterns and colors, the texture and the scent of every flower be a way God communicates his love to me? Maybe the things I recognize as beautiful and good, lovely and honorable are actually the frequency through which God communicates his deep love. Maybe I've been missing the connection all along. Maybe it's time for me to tune in.

And as I start to understand I'm living in a world overflowing with love, it doesn't take long to feel like I'm soaking in it. You and I are being drenched with God's love every day.

When the sky is dancing with color and the hues that form makes you stop and stare.

When autumn leaves have turned such a brilliant red that you wonder if you're having a "Moses moment" and are standing on holy ground.

When you hear a song that moves you to tears.

When you walk into a room and a delicious scent guides your memory to years long past.

When you take that first bite and doubt that anything could ever taste more perfect.

When you're sitting around the table among friends and settle deep within yourself.

When a little one jumps up on your lap and squeezes your neck with squeals of delight.

When your sports hero moves elegantly and effortlessly, and you are lost for words.

When the timing of something is so beyond coincidence that it makes your heart leap.

When the crackle of a fire conjures up memories of good times by the lake.

When you catch the eye of a friend and laugh so hard your tears become sweet medicine.

Every. Single. Thing. We are drowning in love.

To quote singer-songwriter Michael Gungor, "To me, the whole universe is this giant, breathing hymn." Imagine if it's true. The beautiful sunset is about God's deep love for me, not just a demonstration of his grandeur. A savory morsel is God's affection for me, not just about his goodness. The miraculous coincidence is not solely a display of providential power but a gift that shows me he cares. Love is all around and everywhere and these things give me access to feeling his great love for me.

A New Language

In some ways it feels like I've been learning a new language—God's love language. And it is a romantic one that I want to submerse myself in for this journey of transformation. Without it, I'll feel lost, ill-equipped and often downright frustrated. As we'll see in the chapters to come, a whole-heart surrender to God isn't always easy. But understanding that God is good, feeling his love and believing he can be trusted makes the rough patches easier to endure.

I think the advice we hear in Scripture is helpful: "Whatever is true, noble, right, pure, lovely, admirable, excellent, praiseworthy, think about such things." (Philippians 4:8) We're to think about such things because that is where God's love dwells. We think about such things because this is where peace and joy are found and are to be felt. Recognizing them as signs of God's love, we move away from anxiety and fear and towards feeling the abundance of life that truly passes all rational understanding.

I'm getting more proficient at this new love language, but I've got to be honest: there are many days when I feel like a novice. Too often I forget that God's love for me is saturating the world, and I resort back to tamer, thimble-sized versions of his love for me. It's usually in those moments I start to wonder if I should trust him with all the parts of my life, especially the ones I like to control the most.

People often say they know they've hit the next level of learning a new language when they start dreaming in it. I think this is true for God's love language too. God wants to change us from the inside out so this new language of love between us becomes so natural that we can communicate without being tongue-tied. He wants us to be perfectly fluent in his over-the-top love. He's mending what is broken, healing what is hurt and bringing light into those dark places so that I don't need any translation to understand that I am secure and wholly loved. I can't imagine anything more beautiful and abundant than that.

Hitting the Jackpot

God has one direction, one motivation, one gear, one speed and one purpose: love. Writer Brennan Manning explains, "The secret of the mystery is...no matter how great we think [God] to be, His love is always greater." The ferocity of his love is found in the way he accepts me and moves me towards a full, whole life. God isn't in the business of transformation because of duty. He's not reforming me so that he can stomach being in the same room as me. He's motivated by big, bold love and we're soaking in it whether we feel it or not. Being transformed is about capturing and experiencing the abundance that is already ours; this is the great mystery!

Jesus called it the abundant life because it is the type of life that deeply satisfies—and he calls us to that life. He wasn't talking about better TV shows and more vacation. He was talking about healthy bodies and minds, meaningful relationships, purposeful work, other-centered sacrifice, generosity, creativity, beauty, forgiveness and peace. He calls us to the stuff that makes life truly rich.

We learn that the path of transformation is ultimately the path to becoming more like Jesus. He was kind, gentle, selfless, powerful, creative, humble, loving and deeply sensitive to those who were hurting and marginalized.

Who wouldn't want to be like that? A lot of people are deeply offended by Christians. Quite frankly, I don't blame them when I think of the many Christians who have done an absolutely terrible job of following Jesus. But when we look at the real Jesus—the authentic Jesus—most people don't find him offensive. Who wouldn't want to become more like him?

But here's where it gets tricky. As much as we would like to become more like Jesus, we quickly realize that becoming more like him feels like risking the life we hold so dear—life on our own terms. The things that make us feel safe, satisfied, significant and secure are often the things that get in the way of becoming more like him. And Jesus tells us that in order to gain this abundant life we crave, we must lose the life we hold onto so dearly.

That's why transformation feels like a double-dare. Life's greatest dare is to wholeheartedly submit to being transformed by God because it's the pathway to his deep love, to his "yes".

Yes, you are loved and enough.

Yes, love is yours for the taking.

Yes, life is beautiful.

Yes!

TRANSFORM ME

Transform:
to change in form, appearance, or structure; metamorphose;
to change in condition, nature, or character; convert

FROM BUD TO BLOOM

"No, it is not yours to open buds into blossoms.
Shake the bud, strike it;
it is beyond your power to make it blossom.
Your touch soils it,
you tear its petals to pieces and stress them in the dust.
But no colours appear, and no perfume.
Ah! It is not for you to open the bud into blossom.

He who can open the bud does it so simply.
He gives it a glance, and the life-sap stirs through its veins.
At his breath the flower spreads its wings
and flutters in the wind.
Colours flush out like heart-longings,
the perfume betrays a sweet secret.
He who can open the bud does it so simply."
— *Indian Poet, Sir Rabindranath Tagore*

Most people are confused when they find out my favorite season is spring. It's not all that popular where I'm from. In truth, it's the earliest parts of spring that get me giddy. Some people think this is downright strange because there are more gray days than sunny ones. There's lots of snow still lying around that's so dirty it has you wondering what actually fell from the sky all winter long. It's wet and cold and is a far cry from the sand, sunscreen and icy cold drinks of summer.

But there are also days in early spring when I walk out my door and the chilly wind has turned noticeably warmer. Days when I catch a whiff of thawing dirt and see the first red-breasted robin searching for worms still deep in the ground. The sunlight has changed too—it's stronger, hotter and it lasts longer each day. The buds on the trees grow fat, and little green shoots start to poke their heads through the earth. I wear shoes instead of boots. I shovel dirt in the garden instead of snow in the driveway. I start dreaming of new adventures outside.

I love these earliest days of springtime change because it's the visceral reminder that I have survived the cold, quiet winter. Any doubt about whether spring would forget to come has been laid to rest, and I revel in joy knowing great days are ahead. I know that cold temperatures will become warm, heavy snow will turn to rain and buds will bloom. The transformation from winter to spring is evidence that dead things can come alive again. It's time to cash in on everything I've been longing for. That's why I love this time of year.

We all have cold and dead places in our lives, places we need warm winds to thaw. There are things in my life that feel frozen and bound up tight. Even as I hope for a change, I wonder with a measure of doubt whether such places will ever bloom. Sometimes I feel I'll wait in vain for something to change. Hope is buried deep and I'm covered as if with a heavy blanket of snow that seems to hold me back from growing.

But then I get a glimpse of something new changing in me, and I realize it will all turn out okay. I'm reminded once again that transformation is possible. I start to realize that I don't always have to keep my hope for change buried deeply. I can begin to see a new path that leads to a deeper satisfaction than I ever thought possible. I start to believe that I can change, and I grow hopeful for better days ahead.

This is more of a self-hope book than self-help book. There is hope for all of us as we come to know that personal life change—even in the most stubborn places of our lives—is possible. Don't get me wrong when I say self-hope: this is not a book where we put all of our hope in ourselves. I've come to know that getting to the core of my life and making significant change is beyond what I can do for myself. The hope for us is that personal transformation taps into the same power that awakens life out of winter's slumber. While I play my part in my own journey towards a whole life, I'm also invited to embrace the mystery of God at work in me.

Transformation Is Real. Transformation Is Hope.

This isn't a step-by-step guide to transformation either. Transformation is a process, but it's not a formula. Just like any process, there is a general direction in which it's headed but how it happens may look different for each of us. It's a lot like the way flowers grow. All flowers have a process—they bud, then bloom and die—but it's not an exact formula because each flower has its own unique way and timing of growing.

Instead of giving you a formula for transformation, we'll look together at very practical questions like: What is transformation?

Why does God transform me? How does God transform me? What part do I play? What's at stake if I don't? As we answer these questions together, I have no doubt we will feel more hopeful in the One who helps us all.

We'll also explore eight key themes that show us what transformation actually looks and feels like. These themes capture the essence of the life-change process and will be helpful for us as we begin to understand the part we play.

We've already talked about the first theme: transformation begins with God's love. It's the reason why he transforms us. We're going to explore seven more elements, all of which lead to more love. Both the themes and the connections between them are more cyclical than linear.

Take a look at the diagram on the following page. It'll help you see how these themes can work themselves out.

Love always leads to more love.

Let me give you the quick version of how transformation operates:

Life's great dare is to let God transform me. Our transformed life begins with *love* and always leads to more *love*. As I *open* to *surrender* my life to God, I'll embrace the *vulnerability* that comes as I *die* to those things that get in the way and let God do his work in me. I will trust that he will *birth* something new and beautiful in me so I will be *free* to *love* God, others and myself. This is the pathway to abundant life.

Now, let's explore together what that looks like. Let's begin by knowing that we don't have to stay stuck in the bitter cold winter of our lives. Hoping for something to change in the icy parts of our lives is not foolish. Springtime does come and buds always bloom.

OPEN

*"He who is outside his door has the
hardest part of his journey behind him."*

— Dutch Proverb

Many years ago I worked at the best summer camp around (shout-out to *Summer's Best Two Weeks*, and yes, that's the actual name of the camp!). One of my jobs was to guide a group of twelve-year-olds down a river full of Class Two and Three rapids. Now for you white-water aficionados, I know Class Three is small stuff, but I was a newbie and I was working with girls who were eighty pounds soaking wet.

One hot day, we were gearing up to approach one of the tougher rapids on the river. The water was running particularly high that day, so I knew I had to maneuver the raft just right in order for all of us to stay dry.

Put yourself in my raft for a minute. You're barreling down the river toward a monster rapid that's licking the edges of a massive black rock standing five feet out of the water. The sound of the rapids is deafening and your adrenaline is rushing. As we get closer and closer to the rock, from the back of the raft I start yelling, "Lean into the rock! Lean into the rock!"

I bet you're looking back at me like I've lost my mind.

But the only way we're ever going to pop successfully out the other side of the rapid is if all the weight in the raft is on one side—the side where the rock is. Leaning into the rock is counterintuitive, but it's how to get through the rough rapid without capsizing. Each of us has to be open to the possibility that everything will be okay only when we lean perilously close to what feels like danger. It's hard to believe that everything will turn out the way it should if we actually get close to the thing we think will bring us to ruin.

Of course most of the girls decided I was crazy. Only two campers heeded my instructions and leaned into the rock. With predictable precision, the back of the raft got sucked into the swirling rapid. We got tossed into the fast water. It wasn't pretty.

It's the same with transformation. I have to be willing to lean into it. Everything in me may feel it would be much safer to stay comfortable, but avoiding what feels risky will cause more problems than being thrown into a raging river.

Living in the Shallows

Personal change is hard and I've come up with some pretty sophisticated ways (not!) of avoiding it altogether. If I have a bad day, I devour a bag of chips like they're going out of style. When I watch a co-worker get praised for a job well done, too often I go all quiet, feeling like a loser. Instead of dealing with feelings of sadness, I lash out at the people I love the most.

The truth is, we live in a culture that does everything in its power to keep us invested in all the wrong things. We're not given cues to go after a life of meaning and purpose, of healthy relationships and wholeness. Instead, we're encouraged to consume and acquire—to live in the shallows. We don't dive into the deep end and pursue what's most important in life. No joke: if you type "transformation" into any search engine, your screen will be full of selfies, usually of flabby people turned into six-pack-abs-all-stars. I'm not saying this sort of physical transformation isn't important, but digging into a life-change process that has more to do with looking beautiful on the inside is more important (even though it isn't all that popular).

If you're like me, the second I catch a whiff of something in me that may need a little work, I don't lean in. Instead I lean away from it. I binge on Netflix. I waste time dreaming of a prettier life, distracting myself by the stories of others on Facebook. We overwork, over-eat and over-indulge in things that hijack our capacity to reflect on what's really going on inside us. I've never come away from any of that feeling better and these things fracture us away from a whole life.

As my campers learned that day on the rapids, leaning into the harder stuff may be scary, but it gets us to where we need to go.

Sometimes the invitation to being open to transformation comes from being tired of the way things are going and wanting to live differently. At other times transformation has been thrust upon me. Tragedy strikes and I have no choice but to learn how to operate in new ways. I've experienced both. Either way, the door to transformation has been pushed ajar and I've been invited to step past the threshold into a new way of living.

Maybe you feel like you're already living the good life. Even so,

I believe that even the most well-adjusted people have some things that need work. I'm willing to bet when you and I quiet ourselves, our thoughts aren't very far from those places in our lives we'd love to renovate; those places where we'd love to be truly free.

When I quiet myself, I catch a craving for freedom. It happens when I realize how I feel about myself when I step on the scale, or when I'm sitting in a puddle of sadness, wishing my relationships were different. I want to feel free from the heavy guilt I carry and the fear of failure that threatens to bulldoze me off track. What about you? What happens when you get quiet? Where do you long for freedom?

My desire for freedom shows up countless times throughout my day. It pops up when I'm jealous of what other people have, or when I wish I looked different. I long for freedom when I wonder why God put me on the planet, or when I struggle with broken friendships. It comes when I feel frustrated with myself, or when I'm unable to forgive a friend. I want freedom from my addictions and doubt. I'm not sure what's on your list, but each of us has parts of our emotional, physical, mental, sexual and spiritual lives that are trapped and need to be transformed. When we ask ourselves why we do the things we do, we realize we need to address the roots of our behaviors and come to grips with the reality that we don't have what it takes to will our struggles away.

Transformation is the process of being remade into the best versions of ourselves. It's the process of being freed up to receive and give more love. Don't we owe it to ourselves to go there? If God's mission is to make us whole so we can experience his beauty and abundance, then the posture of being open to his action in us is our saying "yes" to God showing us our truest selves.

But being open to this process is a challenge. It feels counterintuitive and we often work very hard to avoid it. Don't we all resist change to some degree? After all, we live our lives a certain way because it works for us. The choices we make give us a sense of satisfaction, security and significance. We hold grudges because it gives us a sense of power instead of feeling the hurt. We indulge in activities that comfort and pacify us even if they aren't all that great for our bodies or our minds. We resist feeling hurt and sad because it often feels like it will destroy us. And the list goes on.

Deciding to eat healthier seems like a great idea until someone bakes you a cake. Agreeing to be more generous with your money feels like a good idea until it limits your ability to purchase that new thing you want. Choosing to be kinder to your co-workers sounds fabulous on the weekends but it's a killer on Monday mornings. Forgiving your mother-in-law is brilliant until she opens her mouth and criticizes you. We act in certain ways because they feel like the best ways to manage and cope with our thoughts, feelings, responsibilities and activities. Change challenges us to lean in, but not being willing to change will sink us.

Get into It

When I was in my last year of university, I signed up for an Outward Bound School in the jungles of Costa Rica. Their motto is "If you can't get out of it, get into it." That should have tipped me off, but it didn't. I had no idea what I was about to get into.

For three weeks, our team traversed a mountain range from 10,000 feet to sea level. We hiked in mud, climbed and rappelled rock faces, camped out by waterfalls and kayaked crocodile-infested rivers—it was both scary and awesome. (You should have seen the waiver we had to sign!) Every day we were challenged in some insane new way. But there was one activity I'll never forget.

One bright sunny day about halfway into the trip, our guides led us into a cave. A cave with bats. A cave with *a lot* of bats. Did you know that in a cave with a lot of bats, there are a lot of bugs? And did you know in a cave with a lot of bats and a lot of bugs there is a lot of...well...bat dung? Seriously. Now, you'd think going into this cave would be the extent of our little adventure that day, wouldn't you? I know I sure did, so I was surprised to find out that the fun hadn't even really begun.

Our guides led us on a twenty-minute hike to a dark cavern at the back of the cave. Then they asked us to hand over our flashlights, our matches and lighters, and even our Indiglo watches. Anything that emitted light was theirs. I've never experienced darkness like that before. It was as if someone took a brush with jet-black paint to my eyeballs. I couldn't blink the darkness away. They told us our challenge was to find our way back out of the cave. We'd have to choose a leader, stick close together and slowly, carefully find our way out. There was no other way to the mouth of the cave. No trick back door, no secret map, no hidden torch to aid us back to the sunlight. If we wanted to get out of the cave, we needed to take a first step regardless of how terrifying and clumsy it felt.

It took twenty minutes to get into that cavern, but it took over three hours to get out. When we finally emerged, we were dirty, a little freaked out and a whole lot happy. I have never been so thrilled to see light! We felt a new freedom once we got out. I didn't have to cling so tightly to my partners or focus so intently on their instructions anymore. We had been stretched but we were better for it. We had moved way out of our comfort zone, through the growth zone and emerged into a free zone. It was totally worth it. Every second we spent groping in the dark was not to be regretted, because every step led us to the light. And it started with one first step.

The Scary First Step

I sometimes wonder if the first disciples knew what they were getting into when Jesus asked them to follow him. How could they have known that saying "yes" in those moments would lead them on an adventure of full surrender, a life of giving up and letting go what was most important to them? For some reason, there was something compelling enough in the invitation to make each of them take a first step. Some of them dropped their fishing nets, others said goodbye to friends but all of them gave up something in order to follow Jesus.

I have a feeling that before Jesus invited them on the journey, they had spent quiet moments thinking life should be different and hoping for some kind of change. It seems they were ripe for the picking. We do know they had been longing to follow someone who would shake things up and revolt against the Roman rule. So when Jesus came up to each of them, the longing for change that simmered just below the surface within them came to full boil. While I don't think they realized the shake-up they longed for would happen in their hearts, they did know that Jesus had what they wanted.

I think that right now many of us are ripe for transformation in significant parts of our lives. I don't think it's a mistake you're reading this book right now. You've been longing for a change and you're looking for a little shake-up. Maybe you've been waiting for a formal invitation. Maybe you've been dancing around the issue, seeing if there's an easier way to get out of it. I'm not sure what your story is, but Jesus is always walking by, stopping to ask us to follow him and inviting us to get into it. He promises to lead us right to the treasure we're longing for.

Do you think any of the disciples, in those early days of following Jesus, ever stopped walking and sat down in the sand feeling confused and discouraged? I do. I think some of them second-guessed their decision to follow him. I bet they missed the comfort of their old lives. I'm sure there were many hard conversations around those early morning campfires about just how difficult it was to stay open to this new way of living. Even though their first decision to follow Jesus was sincere, it would only be natural for resistance and fatigue to set in.

It's the same for us. We can be open to taking a first step—wholeheartedly so. Leaning in toward this treasure always feels compelling in the early moments. We confidently open the door and cross the threshold, hoping for what's to come. But resistance to change is strong. Our desire to being open to transformation is real but it can sometimes be short-lived. It's frustrating, discouraging—but it's also very normal. I've had more moments like these than I can count. I wake up some mornings feeling invigorated with hope of joining Jesus on this journey, and only a few hours later, I'm worn out, defeated and feel like things will never change. Old habits and patterns are so ingrained and their power ties me down. I feel like a chained prisoner who had been running free just a few hours earlier.

Can I just ask all of us to be gentle with ourselves in moments like these? Let's remember we're going after the good stuff. The price is always higher than we expect and takes more effort to acquire—but it's worth it. It's like the difference between the high-end, fair-trade, exotic chocolate you find in specialty stores, and the cheap chalky kind you find in any old place around Easter. Trust me, once we get a taste for the good stuff, it's hard to go back. Once we begin to unearth what this abundant life is all about, we learn that the effort it takes to remain open to transformation is worth it because a transformed life is one that deeply satisfies us in our core.

So what does being open and staying open really look like? Let's get completely practical here. Take a moment to answer these questions. Seriously. Go and get your computer or a piece of paper so you can jot down your thoughts. Put on some music if you need to. Whatever you do, spend some time with these foundational questions.

Here we go: Are you the very best version of yourself right now? And by "very best", I mean are you completely free to love yourself, love God and love others perfectly? Okay, that was an easy question because there is only one answer. It's "no". None of us are completely free because that would mean we are perfect—and, honey, we know we ain't perfect!

Okay, the second question is trickier. It's a two-parter but it gets at the heart of how God might want you to be open to surrender. What's an area of your life where you feel broken or stuck? What might that area look like if it were mended and made whole? Take a moment to be completely honest with yourself. Asking these questions is a powerful first step.

Is it the way you react to your husband? Maybe it's how you talk to yourself as you look in the mirror. Is it fear around your future? How about your relationship with money? Honestly, it could be anything. Maybe you can't shut off work or you try too hard to please people. Regardless of how you answer, God wants to heal what's undone in you so you are freed up and made whole to experience more freedom, peace and love.

Whatever it is, you've just taken the first step. You've accepted the invitation to be open by asking yourself these questions. Can I encourage you to talk to God about what you've come up with? After all, he's doing the inviting in the first place. Coming back to these key questions will be important as you walk through the transformation process.

So, here we go! Our first foot is in that raft. Now let's head downstream. No doubt there are some deeper waters and rougher rapids ahead, but trust me—it'll be totally worth it. We're on this adventure together.

Go ahead. I dare you to lean in.

SURRENDER

*"We must be willing to let go of the life we planned
so as to have the life that is waiting for us."*
— Joseph Campbell

About a million years ago, I was a figure skater. I grew up in a small, rural village and everyone skated. Boys generally played hockey and girls slipped on those white skates to learn how to glide like swans on the icy white.

Every year I would learn a new set of dances—not the jumping, spinning kind, but the ones with a partner and a set pattern of steps we'd learn together. We would execute intricate turns, quick twists and deep edges set rhythmically to the music. One year, my partner was a professional who had been shipped into my small town to help me and some of the other girls who were testing in some of the more advanced dances. He was the expert and had passed these dance tests years earlier. I was going to learn from him in order to showcase one dance for the judges.

My goal was simple but not easy: pass the test. If it had been an option, I would have wanted my pro partner to do the dance all by himself for me—he was far better at it than I was and had proven he knew exactly what to do to be successful. But that's not how it works. I had to learn the steps, we had to figure out how to work together and in order to pass and move onto the next level, we had to maneuver our way around the ice using all the right steps.

The process of learning how to partner together was challenging. The trick was to stick close to each other— closer than what seemed comfortable sometimes. One of the things he had to remind me most often was to lean into him more and to let him guide and move me. The dance only worked when he took the lead and I let go of my control. It felt awkward and counterintuitive. I had my specific steps and he had his, but it never helped my cause to focus on my individual steps alone; it was important that I moved in the context of our connection. The more I focused on my own steps, held control and resisted him, the more labored our dance together became. Sometimes we'd be moving so quickly I was sure we'd fall. All I wanted was to steady myself by pulling away from him.

The day of the test came. Right in the middle of the dance, our blades locked and we fell right in front of the judges. It happened because I was trying to steer us one way instead of melting into where he was leading. I was mortified. I thought it meant an instant failing grade. But without hesitation, my partner took my hand, helped me up off my butt and spoke to the judges on my behalf asking if we could have a do-over. I passed the dance on that day and learned a valuable lesson at the same time.

The dance of transformation is a lot like this. God is clearly the expert. He knows the dance and exactly what steps I need to take to be successful. He guides, encourages and counsels me. The very best thing I can do—even when it feels awkward and unnerving—is to get close and let him maneuver me. He plays his part and I play mine, and we do this dance together. If I don't surrender to the dance, we won't get anywhere. Even when the steps feel unmanageable and frightfully close to a fall, I need to trust he knows what he is doing. God is not the cosmic judge waiting for me to fall. He's my partner who picks me up and helps me when I slip. He wants me to be successful. Letting God change me from the inside out is my chance to partner with someone who wants to see me be my best and knows how to get me there.

The act of surrender is key to the process of transformation. When we long for something to change, we must first let go of the things holding us back. Surrender isn't a one-time event either. It's moment after moment after moment of submitting to the process of loosening our grip on things we like to control. It feels like we're emptying our power and giving up. This is why words like weak, frail, fragile or even pathetic come to mind when I hear the word surrender. But surrender isn't for the faint of heart. It's one of the most powerful and challenging things we'll ever do. It takes great strength. We're being invited to give up our power to control others, to give up manipulating outcomes and to give up comforting ourselves with distraction.

Surrender can look like a lot of things. It can be saying "I'm sorry" to someone you've hurt. It's scanning your budget and admitting you have overspent. It's stepping on the scale and owning the pounds you've gained were of your own making. It's having a good cry, asking your friend for help, forgiving your spouse or praying that God would intervene. Regardless of what it looks like, surrender is an open-handed posture signaling that something has got to change. It's a cue to yourself (and sometimes others) that you're ready to let go.

What do you want to see transformed in your life? How did you answer that question in the last chapter? What's that gap between the best version of yourself and the life you're currently living? Maybe it's a habit, an attitude or a particular fear. Each of those things is like a bundle we think we need to carry in order to have safe and happy lives. I know the bundles I carry help me feel secure and keep discomfort at arm's length. I hold on to resentment so I don't feel the pain of being hurt by a friend. I cling to playing it safe in my work so I don't expose myself to failing at something new. Some of the bundles I carry act as props so I feel significant. I've overworked and kept myself so busy, putting too much value in being "the productive one". Oh yes, these bundles are satisfying because they keep me in control.

But maybe today you and I sense there is something more life-giving than carrying around these bundles. We have an inkling that a full life looks more like running around flying a kite than holding on to things that weigh us down. As we look more closely, we see the bundles as unwanted baggage. We know we cannot run free and hang on to them at the same time. To surrender is to make the choice to let go of power and control and put down the bundles. To surrender is to lay them down in hopes that we'll be able to run free.

Commit to a New Color

One of my favorite authors is Donald Miller. His books *A Million Miles in a Thousand Years* and *Storyline* have been so helpful to me. Both address the idea of building a better life and I'm grateful for the lessons he shares about how to create a more meaningful personal story.

He says that anyone who wants to change his or her life is best served by creating an inciting incident—an event or decision that creates some sort of new reality. He writes, "Once a character is in disharmony, they are suddenly motivated. A human will not be motivated to change until their life is in disharmony. So, if you want to get yourself off the couch, you've got to create an inciting incident that will force you to get up."

Surrender is the inciting incident in the process of transformation. It creates dissonance within us because it's an action that loosens, and eventually releases, our grip on control.

A while back I asked some friends to help me pick paint colors for my house. I had moved into my house six years earlier and had never painted over the beige and yellow tones from the previous residents. I was ready for a change, and nothing transforms a living space more quickly and effectively than paint color. Little did I know a simple request to consult on paint would turn into a fabulous weekend transformation of my entire living space.

It's one thing to hold up paint chips and talk about color at the paint store, and it's another thing entirely to boldly take that first brush stroke and put the paint on the wall. Surrender is like opening the can of paint, dipping the brush in and going for it. It's that first flash of color on the wall inaugurating a change. There's a "point-of-no-return" feeling to it. Hours after we opened that first can of paint, my entire house felt like it had been refreshed. Gone were the marks and blemishes of years gone by. Everything was new and fresh, crisp and clean. Paint color is the silver bullet of home renovation, just as the action of surrender is to life transformation. You can't begin to renovate your life unless you're willing to surrender to a new palette.

Walking the Unknown

I love the story in the Bible when Peter decides to get out of the boat and walk to meet Jesus, who had walked out to the middle of a lake. While we're not entirely sure what got into Peter in the middle of that stormy night, we know he was desperate to join Jesus on the water. Have you ever wondered why?

I'd like to think that Peter, after hanging out with Jesus for a year and a half, was responding to a deep yearning that had been quietly growing within him. It was almost like he couldn't contain his desire any longer. He was desperate to have his relationship with Jesus be as life-altering as the change he had witnessed in so many others who had come to Jesus for help. Less than twenty-four hours earlier, Peter had witnessed Jesus caring for, healing and feeding the large crowds. I wonder whether, as he watched people respond to Jesus, Peter craved a faith that was more robust. Was he feeling desperate for a shake-up? Maybe Peter looked on in envy or even amazement, and knew he wanted more. He wanted something deep within him to be rattled and changed.

Perhaps Peter had been open and longing for a courage that meant something. In those moments on the water when Jesus said, "Do not fear, take courage. I am here," Peter surrendered himself, relinquishing his control. He asked Jesus to tell him to get out of the boat and walk toward him. Peter could have stayed safely and reasonably tucked inside the boat, watching the waves crash around him. He could have held onto his bundle of security a little longer and waited for Jesus to calm the storm. But Peter knew he wanted more. He wasn't forced out of the boat, and didn't have to walk on water, but Peter created an inciting incident by asking Jesus to call him out onto the waves. His longing for a fuller experience of a faith that truly saves was the catalyst for his full surrender and first step.

What happens next is something Peter could not have predicted. Could he really have known that walking on water would work? When Peter scrambled over the side of the boat, he actually started walking on top of the waves. He didn't sink but defied all natural laws and made his way toward Jesus. Imagine the exhilaration and surprise he must have felt. Moments later, as his focus shifted from confidence to fear, from courage back to caution, Peter began to sink and cried out for Jesus to save him. But in those first moments, Peter had gotten a taste of the freedom he'd been longing for. He had experienced the power of faithful surrender and the promise that Jesus would never let him drown. He had a firsthand visceral experience that Jesus could be trusted whether his faith was strong and bold or frail and failing. I wonder how formative this event was in shaping Peter for the things he was going to do in the future. He had accepted the dare and embraced the risk. He had tasted what trusting in Jesus could do. Peter would certainly need to surrender his control and sense of security again and again—but every time he'd step out of his comfort zone he could remember that night on the water.

Putting Down Our Bundles

What gives us the illusion of power and control but at the same time limits our ability to run around free? Whatever it is for you, it's the very bundle God wants you to surrender and let go in order to be transformed.

Maybe you've been hurt in the past and now you limit your connection with people. You hold that bundle of self-protection in order to keep a safe distance and feel secure. Perhaps you overwork and try to make things perfect at the expense of balance and rest. You believe the bundle is what makes you worthy and significant. Or maybe you have an unhealthy relationship with spending money because it brings you comfort and helps you avoid facing your feelings. That bundle is heavy and awkward even though it brings some satisfaction. All our fears, anxieties and sadness show up in many different ways. The bundles we carry bury us and choke out the freedom we crave.

When I think about the times of surrender in my own life, the picture that comes to mind is me falling to my knees, throwing my hands up in the air with a sense of helplessness. I usually get to this point when I've absolutely come to the end of my rope. When I'm tired and desperate for a change. When I want something new to be birthed in me and everything I've tried has left me at a dead end.

Here are a couple of ways this has looked for me.

I was flat-out exhausted, hitting bottom, because I didn't know how to take a break and rest. I was overworking—carrying the bundle of overwork—because I didn't like feeling lonely. The problem was that the more I worked, the lonelier and lonelier I got. Or I'd gain those dreaded winter pounds, making much more than my body feel heavy. I wasn't gaining weight because my metabolism waned like the daylight, but because I was eating my way through the cupboards to hold sadness at bay. The bundle just got heavier and heavier. There have also been times when I go quiet, when I want to feel connection with someone but I'm afraid I'm not worthy enough for that someone to care. I carry the bundle of isolation because the risk of engaging feels too risky. But the trouble then is that life gets radio silent.

There have been lots of times and lots of ways I've backed myself into a corner with no other option but to surrender. I end up hoisting the white flag because I have no other options.

But here's what I'm wondering: Could my surrender to a new way of living be more proactive, like Peter's? Could I see I'm being invited to experience life more fully, and bravely take steps to act on what I really desire, before I start floundering?

Instead of waiting until I've worked myself into the ground, I could acknowledge I'm lonely. Rather than making the potato chip company work overtime, I could admit I'm sad. Or instead of going MIA with my friends, I could tell someone I'm feeling insecure. Could I loosen my grip on the bundles that are preventing me from being free? This is my chance for a great surrender.

I have no doubt that our active surrender will lead to times when we will feel we are in over our heads, sinking quickly with the threat of being overwhelmed. But with each decision to surrender our security for something better, we get a bit more used to feeling vulnerable. We establish some muscle memory of just how to go about relinquishing control. We see the cumulative impact of what happens when we loosen our grip and yield to a process that bears better fruit. We get to see over and over the hand of Someone who is always reaching out for us.

Go ahead. Let's put down our bundles. We were made to run free.

VULNERABILITY

"Have the courage to be imperfect...
Let go of who you think you should be in order
to be who you are. Fully embrace vulnerability,
because what makes you vulnerable
also makes you beautiful."
— Dr. Brené Brown

You know the naked dream? The one where you realize you are the only one in the room without clothes on? This is my recurring dream and it's always set in my first grade classroom. My teacher and all my classmates seem to discover at the exact same moment as I do that I'm not wearing any clothes—I'm totally naked. And horrified. If you've had the naked dream, you know what I'm talking about. You feel total exposure and beg the powers that be to open the floor and swallow you whole. Everyone is staring at your naughty bits and there's absolutely nothing around to cover you up. All you want to do is run but your cement shoes trap you. It's vulnerability on steroids.

Feeling vulnerable is a natural part of life. It's like breathing, really. If you're going to inhale experience, you're going to exhale some vulnerability. You can't participate and engage in living a great life without a bit of exposure. Whether it's starting a new job, going on a date, changing programs at school, having a baby, trying a new hobby or retiring well, living a full and whole life requires that we embrace vulnerability. But so often our first instinct is to run, isn't it? Even a whiff of risk and we feel like we're having the naked dream all over again.

When I take steps toward surrender, I'm doing a shimmy towards the boundaries of my comfort zone. When we feel vulnerable we get in touch with our own fragility and we want to flee. ("Hi there, Vulnerability. Nice to meet you. I'm Comfort. Do you know where the exit is?") This is actually really good. Without this instinct, we could get ourselves into a whole lot of trouble. The adrenaline that accompanies a sense of risk can protect us from really dangerous situations, but it also can hinder us from taking leaps into the unknown. Being vulnerable is as natural to the transformation process as earth is to a garden. You can't have one without the other. If you want something beautiful to grow, you've got to get a little dirty.

I love how author William Ward expresses the value of taking a risk.

To laugh is to risk appearing a fool.

To weep is to risk being called sentimental.

To reach out to another is to risk involvement.

To expose feelings is to risk exposing your true self.

To place your ideas and dreams before a crowd

is to risk their loss.

To love is to risk not being loved in return.

To live is to risk dying.

To try is to risk failure.

But risks must be taken,

because the greatest hazard in life is to risk nothing.

The people who risk nothing may avoid suffering and sorrow,

but they cannot learn, feel, change, grow or really live.

Chained by their servitude they are slaves

who have forfeited all freedom.

Only a person who risks is truly free.

Imagine never laughing or loving, dreaming or caring. When we live well, there's an inherent risk to it all—and the alternative is a form of slavery that leads to a stale, dried-up, monochromatic life.

The Jump

One summer I had the opportunity to go bungee jumping. I was wrapping up three weeks of work in three separate countries in Africa, and was feeling exhilarated by the people I'd met and the things I had learned. Bungee jumping had never been on my list of "must do's", but I love adventure and the time just seemed right. I couldn't think of a more perfect place to take my free-fall either. Soweto, South Africa, overflows with history and is saturated with the call to freedom.

For decades, Soweto had been a place where freedom was just a concept that mocked everyday existence for millions of people as it was ground zero for the oppressive apartheid movement. Even today, it still bears the scars from years and years of unspeakable discrimination. The stories of this city make your heart both swell and break.

On a bright cloudless July day less than twenty years after apartheid officially ended and Nelson Mandela came into power, I surrendered the security of having my feet on the ground and stood three hundred feet high on the top of the iconic Orlando Towers, harnessed by my ankles and prepared to take the leap. The view was profound. In the distance were the gold mines where so many South Africans had worked and lost their lives in order to maintain the economic program of the Afrikaner aristocracy.

The beautiful soccer stadium refurbished for the 2010 World Cup season shone in the sun, witnessing yet another season of struggle and hope for the citizens of this city. And then there was the sea of tin roofs marking the day-to-day challenge for so many families to make ends meet. I couldn't have asked for a more symbolic place to take the leap or a more visceral way to experience these words of Mandela himself: "I learned that courage was not the absence of fear, but the triumph over it. The brave man is not he who does not feel afraid, but he who conquers fear."

The instructions were simple. Shimmy to the platform so that my toes were hanging off the edge, count down fast from five, and on zero, dive headfirst off the platform into the horizon. It sounded simple enough. In truth it actually was. There was nothing terribly difficult or technical about the jump itself, but the rush and challenge of the mental game was something entirely different.

As I was escorted to the edge, the fact I was about to unnaturally hurl myself into midair and plummet to the earth suddenly became very, very real. My fight-or-flight instinct kicked in, and in this case, I wasn't sure I was up for the "flight" option. My mouth got dry. The internal alarm that goes off when my personal sense of safety is at risk was blaring at high pitch. *What on earth am I doing? This is scary! Am I going to be okay?* I knew this was vulnerability's voice, by its tone of caution and excitement. Its pitch was amplified with adrenaline and it was telling me to run and hide. But I knew if bravery were to be victorious, I would have to take the leap. I'm not sure I remembered author Ann Voskamp's exact words while I was standing on top of the platform, but I knew exactly what she meant when she said, "Fear keeps a life small." This jump was big and I wanted to go for it.

I couldn't hesitate. That would lead to nothing good. While hesitating in those moments may feel like it's helping, it really only prolongs the inevitable. I needed to trust all the good work and responsible preparation that had gone into making this jump safe. I took comfort in knowing that thousands had jumped before me. My cheering squad was below, reminding me I could do this. Truth is, if they hadn't been there, I probably wouldn't have been able to jump. Regardless of how vulnerable I felt, I knew I had to muster up the courage and faith, get myself to the edge and go for it. No one could jump for me.

High on the platform, I knew if I was going to jump, I was

going to have to jump afraid.

The man beside me starting counting down fast: five, four, three, two, one—jump! I bent my knees deeply and stared at the farthest point on the horizon. Time both sped up and stood still. I think I held my breath. I dove out off the platform into the void, with three hundred feet of cool bright air separating me and the hard ground below. My natural reflexes kicked in: I squeezed my eyes tight and my stomach found its way to my throat. Free-falling for so many seconds is enough time for your brain to recognize that the situation is unnatural, but in truth, flying toward the earth was exactly where I needed to be. Plummeting through vulnerability into freedom was the weightless exhilaration I was looking for. I wouldn't trade the terrifying sense of fragility if it meant that I had to miss the thrill of feeling so alive!

Our lives are a lot like this, aren't they? We do the hard work of collecting our courage and take steps to the edge between where we have control and where we don't. We're tired of holding the bundles and want things to change. We know we must let go of control in order to fall freely. We may even have people around supporting and cheering us on. And yet, we still feel stuck. We hesitate and wonder what will happen when we let go. We question whether God will stay tethered to us or let us go. We worry we won't make it. This is what vulnerability feels like.

What does it feel like specifically for you? Do you want to follow that notion to change jobs but you're not sure it's wise? Want to trust God with your relationships but wonder if he'll ask you to do something that's hard? Maybe you want to live a more simple life but you're fearful of what people will think. Do you want to stand up for what's right, but it's the unpopular position and you know you'll be mocked? We all want to jump into something we know is better, but when our vulnerability buttons get pushed, we get stuck. We'd rather wait for things to settle, to feel a bit more comfortable before we take the leap. Sadly, our feelings of vulnerability hijack way too many of our jumps.

But here's what I'm learning: when we move through our uncertainty and doubt, the freedom we experience is all the more satisfying. The celebration on the other side of the leap is beautiful and sweet. I know I've missed too many celebrations by hanging on to fear. Feeling exhilaration is feeling fully alive, but it comes at a cost. You see, exhilaration can feel frightening and elating, terrifying and thrilling—all at the same time. It's a rush, but it's not comfortable. It's exciting but not cozy and relaxed. Those of us who generally play it safe (and my hand's up on this one) will have to work harder to get ourselves to the edge.

Jesus Jumped Too

Perhaps one of my greatest consolations is knowing that Jesus has also been there on the edge. This call to vulnerability is something he knows. He never asks me to step into a vulnerability he's not experienced himself.

God broke into human history as an innocent, fragile baby. His finest act was also one of the most vulnerable. Jesus was born, as we all are, completely dependent on someone else to meet every single one of his basic needs. His parents weren't well-off, he was born in hostile conditions and before he turned two his small family was fleeing for their lives. Even before he learned to speak his first words, Jesus lived a vulnerable life.

Jesus had an intimate connection with God. With every step he leaned in to the plans his Father had for him, and at just the right time, Jesus surrendered himself to the greatest mission of all. But his decision to surrender to this mission ushered in significant vulnerability.

We learn that to prepare for what God was calling him to do, Jesus went alone into the wilderness for over a month, with no food to sustain him and nothing to protect him. Imagine it for a moment. Surely the first few days would have been manageable, novel even. But what about day sixteen, or day twenty-four, or thirty-seven? In the wilderness for forty days, Jesus was tempted to cling to things that would seemingly comfort and fulfill him. Satan himself offered satisfaction, security and significance to Jesus—the very things that would completely silence the voice of vulnerability within him.

"Jesus, turn those stones into bread—that will *satisfy* your hunger, won't it?"

"Jesus, hurl yourself off this tower—the angels will keep you *secure*, won't they?"

"Jesus, follow me and these kingdoms will be yours, bringing you power and *significance*."

But Jesus didn't grab any of the bundles he was offered. Instead, he trusted that his Father would give him the power he needed. Scripture tells us that in these moments of surrender and vulnerability, God sent angels to take care of Jesus. God does that for you and me too.

Jesus emerged from the wilderness and declared his mission. Through his own vulnerability, he would rescue the vulnerable. It's ironic, really. God's power in Jesus comes close to the weak and embodies fragility in order to make them strong. Jesus knew the way to freedom was by the path of vulnerability.

Jesus walked with his disciples through towns and villages and spent much of his time teaching others what the abundant Kingdom of God was like. He was casting a vision for what could be and for what was to come. He was also telling people they had access to it now.

The Kingdom is a priceless treasure and it is for everyone to find.

The Kingdom provides an intimate and close relationship directly with God.

The Kingdom comes in power by the path of vulnerability.

Jesus understood that in order for a new way to emerge, the old paradigm had to be dismantled. Something—Someone—must die in order for something new to be born. Jesus had to die in order for new life to come.

As he lived his final days, Jesus experienced the vulnerability of grief that anyone would as he said goodbye to his friends around a table of bread and wine. He felt the vulnerability of loneliness as he sat in a dark garden crying out to his Father who seemed so far away. He felt the vulnerability of rejection when his close friend Peter turned his back on him. He felt the vulnerability of insecurity as Pilate sentenced him to death, and then as he was beaten and mocked by soldiers who didn't even know him. He carried the vulnerability of fear as he stumbled towards the hill on which he'd die hanging naked on a cross. He felt all the vulnerability of loss as he watched his mother moan in grief for her dying son. Yes, Jesus knew everything about vulnerability as he gasped and struggled for his last breath, knowing in those moments he was taking all of our sins to his own grave.

The Kingdom had finally come—and it came because Jesus himself surrendered to the great dare and embraced the vulnerability of God's transformative work.

Over and over again, Jesus put down the bundle of control and faced the vulnerability that came with it. He did it because he knew full alignment with his Father meant full freedom. As we surrender ourselves to what feels like the wilderness, full of vulnerability and the unknown, we can be encouraged by the profound reality that Jesus never asks us to do something he hasn't already done himself.

Experiencing vulnerability is organic to the process of being recreated and reformed. God is changing us out of his great love for us.

I say we take the risk and jump. Even when we are afraid.

DEATH

*"Living aware of your soul's deep longings
can make you feel like you're dying.
Living in denial of them is what can actually kill you."*
— Jonathan Martin

I'm writing part of this chapter hunkered down in a cabin up north by a big lake, where the snow hasn't stopped falling for days. It's the best kind of snow, too. The fluffy kind, light as air. Flakes that look as if they're made of cotton are covering everything thick and white. And it's quiet. So quiet, the silence even rings. If I stand still outside, the only sound I can hear are those big flakes as light as feathers making impact on my jacket. I haven't seen a bird, or a squirrel (or a human being for that matter) for days. Not many months ago this lake would have been bustling with sound—children screaming with glee from the docks, motorboats storming out of the inlet and even the birds and trees would have been singing summer's song. But right now everything is resting and waiting. It appears as though everything of the summer has died and gone for good. It's true—there has been a death of sorts—but we know there is new life hiding dormant, waiting to emerge with vigor. Soon this lake will be buzzing again.

Some things must die to make room for something new.

Selfishness must die to make room for generosity.

Anxiety must die to make room for peace.

Lies must die to make room for the truth.

Pride must die to make room for compassion.

Perfection must die to make room for "enough".

Addiction must die to make room for love.

Fear must die to make room for joy.

Death is integral to transformation. It's the entire point of our surrender. We need to give up something in order to make room for something new. Giving up control means we are putting to death those things we grip so tightly. In truth, they actually have a grip on us. There are things in our lives that need to die in order for us to be freed up to experience the abundant life God is inviting us to.

Will Hernandez, theologian and spiritual director, puts it like this: "Our route to psychological wholeness entails a massive confrontation with our state of brokenness." Dying to our habits, fears and insecurities can feel as foreign and difficult as any death does. We've grown so comfortable with the ways we've been living, gotten so accustomed to the architecture of our lives, that releasing something we've clung tightly to can be painful. We've made our home in the familiar for so long and we don't yet have a map for the new. And this new place—the "death zone"—is a place where we feel helpless and sometimes even hopeless. It feels full of dangerous hazards that threaten to take us out.

Our aversion to death makes sense. Death is awful and scary. The Bible calls death an enemy for a reason. In death, the light of someone's life has been snuffed out. Vitality has ceased and there's only deafening, painful silence in its place. What was warm has now become ice cold; what once was alive is gone forever. Death is ugly because it feels like the end.

At the same time, ironically, death is the hinge of transformation. It's the tunnel to the other side. One of my favorite writers, Eugene Peterson, explains that the whole spiritual life "...is learning how to die. And as you learn how to die, you start losing all your illusions, and you start being capable of true intimacy and love." Making room for something better is contingent on letting something go.

Escaping Captivity

The story of the Israelites being led out of Egypt is helpful to me here. They had lived as slaves in Egypt for over four hundred years. Fifteen generations had known bondage and oppression. They knew nothing different and I'm guessing the invitation to follow Moses into the Promised Land sounded great, even though it was a journey into unfamiliar terrain. Few of them would have been able to imagine the freedom that was before them.

However, their passage out of Egypt seemed to accentuate their slave mentality, even though they were now completely free. Moses was commissioned by God to help emancipate his chosen people, to lead them from slavery to freedom, from death to life.

The call to lay down their old ways of thinking and behaving in order to adopt a new approach as free people was a huge challenge. Had they gotten so used to being enslaved that living in freedom was impossible? It was impossible without transformation. Their old habits had to die before the new ones could be born. I get it completely—don't you? The vision and desire to live as free people is strong but the temptation to feel secure even in things that are destructive can be overpowering.

If you are familiar with the Bible, you know that Moses and his role in leading the people of Israel out of Egypt is an Old Testament foreshadowing of Jesus and his ultimate liberation for us through his death and resurrection. Jesus is known as the Redeemer for a reason: he came to die in order that we may have life. God's grand plan of love is highlighted by this radical reality: the pathway to freedom that leads to abundant life weaves right through the valley of death. You can't get to the full life without spending time in the valley.

Jesus embodies this counterintuitive inversion over and over again. Power is made perfect in weakness. Strength is born from fragility. Gaining your life comes from losing it. Service comes from sacrifice. Life conquers death. This approach is so unfamiliar to those of us who think that a full and satisfying life comes from control, security, power and comfort. Is it really true that in order to find peace and healing, we must relinquish our control and experience a kind of death?

Brennan Manning says, "In order to free the captive, one must name the captivity." What sorts of things are holding you captive? We've talked about this over the past few chapters. What habit, what pattern, what approach to life are you sensing God wants to transform in you these days? Let's name what's keeping us captive from a beautiful and abundant life. These are the things we are holding on to—and need to surrender over and over again. It's in letting these things die that God is able to inject his power and renewal. It's hard to see that when you're feeling vulnerable and unsure. It's difficult to trust that something better could actually emerge as you let go of what's worked and seemed comfortable. Hanging out in the death zone is hard but there is a promise of rebirth waiting to burst everything wide open.

Hanging in the Death Zone

Let me give you an example of what living in the death zone has looked like in my own life.

Years ago, I was dating a guy I thought I was going to marry. We were both in our early thirties and, after three years of being together, we found ourselves needing to make a decision to either get engaged or break up. What happened, you ask? Let me just say there's no ring on my left hand. We decided to end our relationship and do the hard work to untangle our lives from each other, to imagine and live our lives apart.

Those first few weeks and months were torture. I felt like I was both caged in and coming out of my skin all at the same time, like I was in withdrawal from a powerful addiction. Because our parting was mutual and respectful, I didn't feel rejected or angry. I just felt a deep sadness about letting go of a person I loved.

I knew that I needed help. I needed to heal from this loss. I needed to change my mental and emotional habits. I needed to get comfortable in my skin as a single person instead of a woman on track to getting married. I needed to be transformed. That's what I've found: often our desire to be transformed comes out of those places where we feel our deepest needs.

I had a choice to make. I could stuff down the feelings and find a quick replacement that would offer cheap comfort, or I could open up my hands to let go of control, embrace the vulnerability of feeling the pain and let God heal what was hurting. I could cover up the sadness and pacify myself by grabbing on to some sort of counterfeit security, or I could open myself up and walk through the shadows for a while.

The problem is that surrendering to what's uncomfortable feels dangerous. Walking into the unknown makes us feel insecure. I had to get in touch with just how sad I really was; there were lots of tears and feeling lost. The process of surrendering meant weeks and months of slowing down my pace so I could reflect and mourn. It involved facing the fear of being single again.

Do you know what would have felt better and easier in those moments? Pushing down the painful feelings and denying that they even existed. Replacing sadness with bitterness—reframing the story so I could actually hate him instead of praying for him. It would have been easier to distract myself with other things that gave me pleasure. You can see why walking through the valley is difficult. It doesn't gratify us instantly. It doesn't feel safe and comfortable. It feels like at any moment our emotions could ambush us and we'll lose ourselves completely. We don't want to walk through this minefield, we just want to get over it and move on.

I'm Not a Masochist

Embracing "death" gets us in touch with our fragility and powerlessness like nothing else does. It wasn't something I always wanted to do. There were many days when I walked a tightrope between denial and embrace. I certainly didn't have a flawless record of surrendering fully into those vulnerabilities. Some days I was living in full denial, while at other times I got closer to vulnerability and willingly tasted the flavors of suffering.

Before you get the wrong idea, you should know that I'm not a masochist. I'm Dutch and—trust me—we have our own set of issues (we're driven, stoic, rational, utilitarian), but loving pain isn't one of them.

Choosing to avoid pain is choosing to deny the opportunity for God to heal us and bring us to a new place. If we don't surrender to the vulnerability of death, we will be stuck in a place that forever limits our taste of a full, beautiful, healed life. We see this demonstrated so well when we lean in and look closely at what God was doing on the cross. God's plan is to bring us to a new place and show us that his great love included suffering and death.

God didn't conquer sin and death and usher a new way of love by triumphantly overcoming the enemy with power. He did it through a suffering love.

When Jesus suffered, he showed us that the pathway of transformation can include pain. This can be hard for me to swallow. After all, I'm addicted to being comfortable; I crave instant gratification; I have a raging sense of entitlement; and in many ways I'm immunized against personal growth. Wouldn't you put yourself in that camp most days? If the essence of transformation is more like the downward mobility of sacrifice and letting go of our power, it's no wonder we have such an aversion to it. The topic of suffering is not an easy one. We often want to find out the reason behind our suffering instead of searching for the meaning in our suffering. There's a difference.

Famous psychiatrist Viktor Frankl explains that if we cannot find meaning in our suffering, we will despair. He saw firsthand in the Nazi concentration camps the striking difference between those who were able to find some meaning in their suffering and those who could not. People who could not find meaning in their suffering were more likely to commit suicide. But suffering isn't an end in and of itself. We don't suffer for suffering's sake, and neither did Jesus.

Let's take a moment to consider suffering in the context of our transformation. Jesus talks about dying to our own ways in order to follow him and experience the fullness of the Kingdom life. Let's take our cues from the Apostle Paul in Scripture. How did he understand suffering and why does he seem so motivated to embrace it?

Paul knew that there is no way of avoiding pain in this life. He knew that pursuing the treasure of the Kingdom life would mean encountering major obstacles. He also seemed to know that the pursuit of a life that completely satisfies requires suffering, although the suffering can be used for good purposes. He grasped that the suffering he would encounter would help transform him and enable him to become the best version of himself.

Chris Heuertz, author and contemplative activist, says, "Suffering is the midwife to maturity." Paul knew that God transforms us and helps us become more mature so that we can experience his perfect love. Paul trusted that any suffering he endured would somehow be used for good and not be wasted. Becoming more and more like Jesus means following where he leads, and Paul knew this would mean sharing in some of the suffering Jesus had endured.

In his suffering, Paul experienced intimacy with Jesus. It certainly wasn't the only way he experienced Christ's love and power, but suffering helped him connect with Jesus in a way like no other. Priest and author Richard Rohr calls this kind of experience transformative dying, and explains that "Jesus' big message [is] that there is something essential that you only know by dying—to who you think you are! You really don't know what life is until you know what death is." I think the Apostle Paul knew that without suffering he couldn't (and we can't) know about the love and power of God. Again, it's not the reason why we suffer that matters as much as the meaning we can find in our suffering.

Paul makes a strong case for how our burdens and weaknesses help us experience Christ's power and strength. It's when we are at the end of our rope that we understand God's grace most profoundly. When we feel like we are close to ruin, we are in a place to be comforted. Paul explains, "We always carry around in our body the death of Jesus, so that the life of Jesus may also be revealed in our body." (2 Corinthians 4:10) Aren't things always sweeter and richer when we need them more? Isn't a cold glass of lemonade more satisfying when you are thirsty? Doesn't a great promotion feel more rewarding when you really had to work for it?

Paul was acutely aware of how much he needed Jesus and walked into suffering (rather than avoiding it) time after time as a pathway to intimacy with him. Paul didn't chase pain but found deep meaning in it. You and I are invited to do the same. He says,

"But whatever were gains to me I now consider loss for the sake of Christ. What is more, I consider everything a loss because of the surpassing worth of knowing Christ Jesus my Lord, for whose sake I have lost all things. I consider them garbage, that I may gain Christ...I want to know Christ—yes, to know the power of his resurrection and participation in his sufferings, becoming like him in his death, and so, somehow, attaining to the resurrection from the dead."
— *Philippians 3:7, 8, 10, 11*

The truth is that my motivation for writing this book was rooted in my personal experience with deep suffering. There was a traumatic season in my life when I was facedown in the death zone, suffocating under the weight of pain with no hope of a rescue and no hope of new life. I lived with—and agonized over—very real questions: How can anything beautiful come out of such pain and brokenness? How can life and love emerge from my life when everything has gone cold, dark and dead? How do you keep going when hope is buried deep? As I asked those questions, I've come to learn that the darkness of suffering and death can be a hinge that swings us open to bright, new life.

My story is mine—no greater or more important than anyone else's—but it's a story to remind us that God never ever leaves us for dead. His love is too big and his faithfulness too bold. I will tell you about a very significant transformation I experienced, about how I know death is never the period at the end of a sentence and that there's always something more beyond the shadows and the valley. Let me tell you how lame stories can be made grand, tired characters turn heroic and hopeless, stale tales can shine bright with new life.

STARLESS NIGHT. MORNING LIGHT.

"Then their shining stopped, for they left the sky,
and you, O God, left with them.
And I am left alone beneath a starless sky with
a starless heart that barely beats."
— Ann Weems

I was sitting in the dark. The sun had set and I hadn't turned on any lights. The phone rang. It was my surgeon calling with the results.

"Now, Christa, you should write down what I'm about to tell you," he said. "You have something called Hodgkin's Lymphoma. That's cancer. I want to make sure you know before I go away for Christmas holidays."

H-O-D-G-K-I-N-S. I wrote it down. I don't think I had ever heard the word before. I did know what cancer meant, though, and that was all I really needed to hear. That doctor knew what he was doing when he asked me to write it all down because those moments in the dark after I hung up the phone were a swirl.

God.

Help me.

How am I going to tell my family?

What am I supposed to do?

Shit. I have ten girls from my youth group coming over in thirty minutes for a sleepover.

With denial in full force, I welcomed those hyper girls into my apartment for an evening of Christmas movies and popcorn. It wasn't until after midnight when the girls were asleep that I let myself feel sick to my stomach with fear of the unknown. For the first time in my life, at the ripe old age of twenty-four, I realized that my life was fragile, that it could all come to an end before it had really gotten started. Worse still, was the anguish of knowing I'd have to tell my family and friends. In those moments, I was more anxious about ruining people's Christmas than about the cells in my body that had gone rogue.

Less than three months earlier on my twenty-fourth birthday, I had written in my journal about something that I hoped for: *"So, 24 – here I come! I hope I continue to grow to be more like Him who is in me."*

Little did I know the direction the answer to this desire would take. I certainly wasn't anticipating something that would bring me to my knees and rock my world forever. How could I have known what was coming in the months to follow?

My life up to this point had been pretty charmed, not perfect but good. I had a happy childhood with two parents and a younger brother, Todd, who loved me. We were the perfect playmates, born just eighteen months apart. We grew up in an idyllic village in rural Ontario where I knew every street corner and the best places to play hide-and-seek. My high school and college years were marked by a deepening faith in God, lots of fun and wonderful opportunities to learn and lead. I had lots of friends and bright optimism for my future. I was settling into my first job in a church in New York, excited about sharing my life with junior and senior high school students. Life was exciting; I knew I was in my prime.

Following my diagnosis and throughout my treatment I vigorously recorded all my thoughts, chronicling those first few months: toxic chemo; losing all my hair; how I was experiencing God; all the questions I had about my future. I wanted to capture my thoughts and ideas as a way to bear witness to the incredible events that were unfolding in my life—writing it all down was a lifeline for me. Being a lethargic, inactive patient was a very different lifestyle than I was used to. And while I struggled alone in my apartment with the day-to-day side effects of treatment, I endured, knowing this cancer thing was going to be wrapped up by summer. By the time I hit my twenty-fifth birthday in September, it would be a thing of the past and I'd have a new story to share.

At least that's what I thought.

I had no idea this would be the year the bitter cold of winter would kill and freeze everything up tight. I could never have anticipated that spring would forget to come.

~

Ding-dong. "Who the heck is ringing my doorbell at seven-thirty on a Thursday morning?" I asked myself, as I lay sick in bed.

I looked out my window to see who was at the front door. I saw

Gary and Alice, my "surrogate parents" in town, and then I noticed my dad was with them. I was furious.

"Why on earth would Gary and Alice tell my parents I was sick in bed with an infection? I'm fine," I thought as I put on my ball cap instead of my wig. "Now my dad has driven three-and a-half hours in the middle of the night to check and see if I'm okay."

I walked down the stairs to the front door, putting on my happy face. As I opened the door, I saw my dad's friend standing beside him. It was a whole "Save Christa" contingent, coming from Ontario to New York.

As I stood in the threshold of the door, I looked at everyone and asked with a hint of frustration in my voice, "What are you all doing here? I'm feeling *fine!*"

Dad stared deep into my eyes. "Christa, I have to tell you some very bad news. Todd died yesterday. It was a car accident."

In those moments on that crisp April morning, less than four months after I was diagnosed with cancer, my whole world collapsed.

It stopped. It died.

The Painful Collapse

When I think back to that time, I still find it very difficult to put into words. Something significant broke in me that day. Something so core and central shattered into a million little pieces. When I think about the story of my life, I see it in two distinct segments: life before April 7, 1999, and life after. And it's more than just life with or without Todd. It's a much bigger divide, impacting the deepest parts of my spiritual and emotional core. It's also the place of the most profound transformation within me.

The months that followed were the most excruciating I've ever experienced. With every passing day, I became physically weaker and experienced painful side effects from the chemotherapy and radiation. There was agonizing loneliness from spending hours incapacitated and alone in my apartment. There was no social media to console, distract or make connecting with others easier. I was left haunted by my thoughts and the searing ache of loss. As the months on the calendar turned, I found myself emotionally unraveling and losing myself; each month seemed to find me buried deeper in the pit. I could feel myself shutting down. Life grew silent—it was deafening and terrifying. This sickness, this death, this heartache was choking the faith and hope right out of me. All the color in my life was draining away. I wasn't grasping for my life with courage. Instead, I was quietly fading away. All comfort and joy were dismantled and I felt empty-handed, boxed in, all alone, dissolving into the dark.

Grief that comes from deep loss can be incredibly confusing and disorienting. The most painful part was my deep sense that God had completely abandoned me. The solid ground I had stood and built a life on was now gone. Every step felt like it could be my last, like the earth beneath me could give way, swallow me up and I'd never be found again. My heart was cut raw with grief. It was as if the million little pieces of my shattered life were daggers, slicing me thin. The fear of having to live this tortured life was so overwhelming. Deep sadness spilled out of me, and all over my understanding of who God was in times of trouble. I could not carry the weight of the pain. I thought God—in whom I had placed my trust—had sucker punched me. He couldn't deal with my sadness and left me on my own in the dark to drown.

At least that's how it felt.

I remember stumbling across this poem by Ann Weems. It captured the agony I was feeling so well. I sent it to friends just a few months after Todd died.

O God of my heart,
it is your name I call when the stars do not come out.
O God of my soul,
it is to you I turn when the torrents of terror drown me.
O God of mercy,
it is for your hand I reach when I stumble on stones of sorrow.
O God of justice,
it is to you I cry when the landslide of grief buries me.
I stand beneath the night where stars used to shine and
Remember gazing mesmerized at the luminaries of the sky
Until I could walk the ink-blue beach between their shining.

Then their shining stopped, for they left the sky,
and you, O God, left with them.
And I am left alone beneath a starless sky
with a starless heart that barely beats.

Will your stars never shine again?
Will they never again speak of your mystery?
Will they never again sing their songs to my soul?
Will I never again know the wonder of the God of star and sky?

O God of my heart, peel back the night
and let the starlight pour out upon my upturned face.
Let my eyes drink a sky of stars.
Let my heart bathe in the stunning light until my soul
sings again with the conviction of the faithful.
In your mercy and justice, O God of my heart, call me by name,
And the stars will shine once more
as they did on that morning when they first began to sing.

— *Ann Weems*, Psalms of Lament

Long days alone turned into longer weeks and months. On my last day of treatment, ten months after I first went to the doctor, I stood in the small dressing room cubicle, and put on my clothes after my last zap of radiation. I stared at the girl in the mirror. I gazed into my stale, gray, sullen eyes, and was shocked at how damaged I looked. I didn't recognize myself. My body had changed dramatically over the months. My heart had grown so dim, heavy with all the sorrow. My spirit was empty and dark. I was completely broken—all the music had stopped, all the lights had gone out. Long gone was the energetic, happy, faith-filled girl who was hopeful for her future. I had all but died. I was a smoldering wick, close to being snuffed out completely. The smoke that rose from the ash of my life was a cruel reminder of the bright light that once was.

I wrote in my journal: *"I'm done treatment. I hardly recognize myself. What an insane and painful year. How do I move on from here? I used to turn my face to the sun and smile. Before, the wind dancing on my back would make me laugh. But now all my breath has been stolen, and all my joy is gone."*

Have you ever had a season in your life when you felt like you couldn't catch your breath, when every single drop of joy completely evaporated? Have you had the experience of feeling mocked by the things that once brought you peace and purpose? Ever had questions that haunted you and answers that never came? Felt so desperate for some sort of personal rebirth that you knew you would die if you didn't get it? What followed my final day of treatment was a very long season of grappling with the intense pain of my life and the struggle I had with God. You can't reflect on the process of transformation without having a sense of your starting point. Mine was a very, very low one.

The process of rebirth and renewal took a very long time. To be honest, there was a long season where I wasn't ready to be open, to really dive in to the boxing ring with God. I felt like I was going to have to duke it out with him, and I knew I didn't have it in me. I was so fragile and fearful I would discover I had lived a fraudulent sucker-of-a-life following Jesus. That I'd realize all the stakes I had put in the ground with God would get pulled up, and all I'd be left with was a deflated, collapsed life. I was committed to finding out what was really true, but I had to wait until I knew I could handle whatever the outcome would be. I had to be prepared to walk away from it all. I had to be prepared to say goodbye to God, walk out the door and never look back.

During that time, I saw a professional therapist and stuck close to friends. Friends cried with me and for me. The tears we shed were messy and cleansing all at the same time. As I look back, it was moments like these where God showed me his grace and comforted me. I couldn't see it at the time, but that is what it was. Now, I can see how God wove an incredibly beautiful bond between my friends and me; ironically he used the thread of pain and tragedy. He's like that, you know: he takes the ugly and awful and turns it into something unexpectedly beautiful. He's the only One who can do that sort of thing.

During this time God just waited. He wasn't threatened by my questions, my angry pleas for answers or my lack of trust in him. Rather, he patiently and lovingly protected me by putting specific people in my life; orchestrating strategic, timely conversations; and giving me the gift of time to work things out with him. For me, it felt like a wrestling match. But over the years I can see that it really has been more like a safe, comfortable conversation with someone who would never leave. God sticks it out with us as we wander and wonder about who he is and how much he loves us. I think Spanish philosopher Miguel de Unamuno y Jugo had it right when he said, "Those who believe that they believe in God, but without passion in their hearts, without anguish in mind, without uncertainty, without doubt, without an element of despair even in their consolation, believe only in the God idea, not God Himself."

Perhaps the most significant transformation I experienced was the dramatic unraveling and rebuilding of my understanding of God. As I re-read my journals and remember that time, it's very clear to me now that my understanding of who God is during times of crisis and pain was completely underdeveloped. Chalk it up to the innocence of youth, my inexperience with profound loss and some weak theology. My understanding of a loving God didn't jive with the pain I was experiencing: it just didn't fit.

I had believed that the absence of pain and suffering indicated the presence of God, and that the peace, joy and comfort God promises would come when suffering was absent. In my season of suffering, I put the sovereign nature and goodness of God on trial, and found God guilty because I was experiencing such intense pain. I wanted to spit in the faces of the people who told me Jesus was weeping alongside me. I felt like I was being mocked. How could this be true when it felt like God had completely left the building? I spent months and months questioning him, recording my agony in my journal when I could:

How can you be weeping with me and at the same time feel so far away? If you are really comforting me, why am I so miserable?

If I'm to have joy and peace in my suffering, why do I feel like the only thing I'm doing is surviving?

Why does it feel like you've completely abandoned me instead of rescuing me when I need you the most?

I don't need you to take the sadness away; I just want to know you care. I just want to know you're there. I can't believe you've left me like this.

Today, I am able to see things more clearly. I'm able to have a clearer perspective that isn't overwhelmed and distorted by such heart-ripping sorrow. I have come to realize that God was not walking away from me. Rather, I needed to walk away from who I thought God was.

Putting the Pieces Back Together Again

My pain was too big for the God I had come to know. I could no longer have a relationship with that version of God. I needed to deconstruct my understanding of God in order to rebuild a more durable, more accurate understanding of who he actually was—one that fit with my experience. I had to leave him—or at least my understanding of him—and unravel everything I knew.

This was a tremendously lonely and confusing process. When you've deconstructed everything and the blocks of what you believed are scattered, it feels like there is nothing to cling to. Anything I had relied upon was smashed to pieces and that was why it had felt like God had left the room. That's why it felt like I was drowning in the dark under a starless sky with no one to rescue me.

It took many slow, difficult years to really understand that he hadn't abandoned me, and to build a richer, more robust understanding of God. In many ways, I did say goodbye and walk out the door. Once I had a more accurate understanding of God, I found a new door to walk through, and began to recognize his deep compassion and how he comforted my broken heart.

As I think about the years since that time, I can only describe my transformation as a *slow miracle of God. Slow* because it took years to really have some of those very broken pieces mended and made whole. *Miracle* because miraculous is the only word to describe my experience of going from essential destruction in body and spirit to thriving and being full of gratitude. *Of God* because only he who can do such a thing. I certainly couldn't, nor could you. Honestly, there were many, many months filled with empty days and painful hours of wondering if God was gone forever. Transformation is literally coming back from the dead—life rising from the ash. Only God can do that.

I believe death will never have the last word. I believe death died once and for all when Jesus swallowed it up on that Roman cross and showed us all that life really does reign. Death to life is the hinge in the grand story of all of our lives. Author Barbara Brown Taylor says that "new life always starts in the dark." Whether it's a seed planted in the dark soil, a baby growing in the quiet of the womb or the blossoms of the apple tree lying dormant in the cold, life begins to show its miraculous power only after death. It's true for you and me too.

We are never left in the pit of death. There's always a new day waiting because God is making all things new.

All. Things. New.

Rebirth

"The lotus flower blooms most beautifully
from the deepest and thickest mud."
— *Buddhist Proverb*

About ten months after my brother Todd died, I was living at home and struggling to cope. I ached for the life I had known before Todd died and I got sick. I longed for the "old me". I felt so disoriented and disheartened about who I really was and who I was becoming. I was sad, distant and unsure. I knew so much of me had died: my innocence, my health, my hope and confidence and my "upward mid-twenties trajectory"—it was all gone. I wasn't even a sister anymore. There was no question about what had been destroyed. I felt like I was at ground zero and starting from scratch.

I can count on one hand the number of times in my life I've had a dream I knew God had infused straight into me. One cold, snowy night, just a month before the first anniversary of my brother's death, I had one of them. This dream changed me.

In the dream I was a tree. I was a strong, healthy pine tree with deep roots that reached far into the earth. The tree was suddenly and horrifically cut down to the ground. Its beauty, vitality and grace were cut right down. It was dramatic and traumatic. Nothing remained that once was—no stump, no branches or pinecones, nothing. The only thing left intact were the roots that were still deep within the ground, hidden from sight.

Then, slowly and quietly, out of the ground from the pine's root system, a small, tender, fragile shoot began to grow. First, one fresh, green baby leaf popped out, then two...and three, until the small tree had hundreds of soft, small, translucent leaves. I was no longer a pine tree—even though my deep pine roots were still intact—but had been reborn into something completely new. The tree and its leaves were as delicate as paper and vulnerable to the elements, but it was alive and growing. The trauma of its destruction had not annihilated it completely even though it should have been demolished beyond repair. Even in its seeming death, new life was somehow burgeoning. Something completely unexpected was being fashioned. And with every new leaf that burst open, the hope that the tree would survive was confirmed. It was pure miracle. How could a destroyed pine tree transform into a thriving tree with thousands of emerald leaves?

I remember waking from that dream feeling like I had experienced something significant. I didn't know exactly what it all meant, but I knew it was from God. I was desperately trying to discover who I was and how to live after such life-altering traumas. I knew that deep down there must be some parts of me left intact, even though nothing in my life really showed it. How I felt about myself, God, other people and my future had completely changed, and none of it really made any sense to me anymore. But God was still making a way forward for me. Each leaf represented a new experience I was having as the "new Christa", the "post-destruction Christa". I felt completely different and incredibly fragile, but with each new opportunity and experience, a new leaf bloomed.

A new leaf would open when I was asked how many siblings I had—how was I to answer that now? Another popped out when I found myself laughing out loud for the first time. Was I allowed to do that? Would laughing make people think I wasn't sad anymore? Leaves showed up when I started to look for work again or considered going back to my graduate studies. I was discovering what my "new normal" was. I was learning what my life would feel like as a cancer survivor and as a sister without a sibling. I was uncovering new strength.

Long gone were the pine needles and cones that marked my old understanding of reality. In its place there was a new young tree, receiving its life from the same source, yet presenting itself so differently in the world. Rebirth takes some getting used to. If we're gentle with ourselves, we'll discover we are becoming more beautiful now than we ever imagined possible. This new life is full of the grace we need to keep moving forward on the uncharted path.

One of the best gifts I've ever been given was from friends who commissioned an artist to paint this dream of mine. This painting hangs on a white wall in my office. There are fiery oranges, rob-in-egg blues and the most perfect green depicting the new leaves. My favorite part of the painting is the dark black trunk of the tree. There, at the bottom of the trunk where tree meets ground, is the silhouette of a girl hunched over. But it's not what you think. She's not huddled in pain, suffering from a blow to the gut, trying to catch her breath. No, there is grounding going on in her. Like she's composing herself, gathering strength from the roots below her, praying as one who's about to emerge with the hope of flourishing. I remember being that girl. It didn't feel like strength at the time, but it was.

While we wait for the next season to come, the better season, we can remember the deepest root who grounds us—Jesus. Surviving the death zone (whatever it may look like) and being renewed takes courage, but we're never left on our own. Our strength comes from a much deeper source.

Lessons from the Caterpillar

I've never had a baby, but you don't need to be a mother to know birth is a miraculous thing. Seriously, it's unbelievable. Brand-new dads walk out of the delivery room wide-eyed with delight; they've been shocked-and-awed by God himself. Courageous mothers are overwhelmed when they meet for the first time the gift that grew within them. At birth we usher in the brand new, the untouched, the pure and the perfect.

But rebirth folks—now this is truly miraculous! There should actually be a new word for it—it's something beyond a miracle really. Rebirth means something was once dead and has now come back to life in new form. Something was broken, tarnished and warped, and now has been remade into something whole, beautiful and lovely. We don't have many examples of this sort of thing. Rebirth is rare and powerful.

Consider the butterfly for a moment. I bet there's something about butterflies you didn't know.

As you *do* know, a butterfly isn't actually born a butterfly; rather it starts out as a caterpillar. But its colorful wings are not somehow trapped inside the wiggly worm's body waiting to be freed:

there are no wings. They don't grow over time on the caterpillar's body either. They simply don't exist.

A young caterpillar's main job in life is to eat and shed its skin. (It also tries not to get eaten by bigger creatures!) It's destined for greater things, though. I'm not sure if it really knows it, but there is something deep within itself, something hard-wired into its DNA that urges it to be reborn into something entirely new. It must submit to a process that will bring the life it knows to an end in order for a new one to emerge. Over and over, it eats and sheds its skin, and eventually the caterpillar comes to the point where it needs to shed its skin one last time. But on this final occasion, things are different. This time everything changes.

The caterpillar finds a branch and hangs upside down. It doesn't really do anything other than wait on the process that is happening within. It doesn't eat and it barely moves. It hangs out like this for days, completely exposed to the threat of being eaten by predators, and very vulnerable to being destroyed. Eventually, its skin splits, but this time something inside takes over—as the young caterpillar wiggles, its dead skin shrivels up and a harder chrysalis shell envelops its whole body.

But here's the crazy part! The caterpillar doesn't just sit in this chrysalis shell and grow wings. The thing actually *dies* inside itself. The same digestive juices that once processed food now basically attack and kill the caterpillar. In some ways it eats itself from the inside out. The caterpillar must die. But there are some "sleeper cells" left intact, DNA that activates to grow an entirely new body, one with brilliant colors and strong wings. The death process is actually the birthplace for something beautiful to begin.

After days in the cocoon, the young butterfly emerges with the same struggle and fragility as the birth of a baby. It doesn't come out the same way it went in. It's been dramatically changed and now reflects something that's always been a part of itself, something that was hidden during its caterpillar phase. It's tentative at first, trying to get used to this new way of being, trying to adjust to having wings and the urge to fly. Did you know that when the butterfly first makes an appearance, its wings aren't quite ready? After climbing out of the chrysalis, the butterfly must immediately pump fluid into its wings in order for them to expand to full size. It then rests for a few hours to allow its fragile wings to be completely prepared before it takes its first flight. Then, it stretches those beautiful wings and launches off to its new life as a butterfly. There is a new normal to get used to, but the process is totally worth it because it's finally free, having matured into its true identity.

This whole process is known as metamorphosis. *Meta* means "to change" and *morph* means "form". Transformation is about changing our form, too. Do you know what they call this last stage in a butterfly's life? It's called the imago stage. Imago: "in the image of". A butterfly is not considered adult and mature until it reaches this stage. Like us, it's only when we submit to the process of being transformed that we mature to our true identity: who we really are and how we've been made in the image of our Creator. Our old habits and patterns die and we are reborn to the more mature and whole version of ourselves. We are re-formed to reflect more of the beauty of God and to live lives of abundance.

The truth is, we are never really done transforming. We are always both the caterpillar and the butterfly. We have parts that are healing and parts that have been healed. There are parts that are a work in progress and parts that have been made new. We will live in this cycle until the end of days, when all things in creation are finally redeemed and made perfect. That is when our transformation will be complete.

Re-birthday?

How do we know when certain parts in us are re-formed? How do we know when our re-birthday is? Are these even the right questions to be asking?

Knowing exactly when we've been reborn isn't easy: there's no happy face sticker on the calendar telling us that "death" is over. We often can only see certain things have died (or are dying) in us when we look back on our lives. We realize old habits no longer have the same control over us. Things that brought us anxiety have been replaced with peace. Where there once was confusion, there is more clarity. Joy seems to have emerged from fear and sadness. We can't say for sure when things changed, but we know they are different. God has done in us what only God can do. It's all grace.

I once had a friend tell me something I've never forgotten. He said those of us who follow Jesus need to look at our own transformation as simultaneously having three parts:

I *was* saved and transformed into a new creation.

I *am being* saved and transformed into a new creation.

I *will be* saved and transformed into a new creation.

Author Dallas Willard explains that spiritual transformation is not behavior modification. Rather, it addresses the roots of our behavior. Transformation is not just a winning over the will, but it's a healing and rewiring of our mental, emotional, physical and spiritual maps. It's an inside-out job that happens through the Spirit of God at work in us. This rewiring is most often gradual and takes time. It's incremental with stops and starts, diversions and sidetracks. Maybe that's why we call it a journey. Every step is into new territory; it's no wonder we sometimes feel quite fragile or lost.

I think the feeling of being reborn within the transformation process can also feel a bit like those first few moments when you wake up from a nightmare. You feel completely discombobulated. Your body is heavy, your mind is confused and your heart is weak with the reverberations of fear. You lie in bed, still breathing heavy with alarm. As the seconds pass and you slowly return to reality, you feel as though a truck has hit you. After a few moments, you wiggle your fingers and toes, blink a few times and a wave of sweet relief washes over you because you know it was just your imagination. You're not sure what to do next, and so you just lie there, letting your breath push back any remaining darkness that lingers in your mind.

After we experience the process of dying to ourselves, there can certainly be an awe-filled appreciation for being awakened to a new reality, but there's also a keen sense of our fragility as well. We are tentative, because we feel the dark shadows of old habits lurking around the corner, tempting us to do things the way we used to. There is a faint echo of fear off in the distance, threatening us with our old way of living. Even though the promise and potential of what lies ahead is far more compelling, we are tentative, wondering how to try on this new way of living. We are comfortable with "normal", yet there is nothing normal about this new experience. Being reformed is essentially the start of a journey to find a "new normal". If you really wanted to boil it down, the entire transformation process is the work of dismantling the old in order to uncover and live out of the new. Rebirth is step number one in the journey of all things new.

Walking the Unfamiliar

During the times in my life when an old habit or pattern is being put to death, I almost always feel fragile. I'm not exactly sure where and how to step. I'm so used to carrying the bundles. I've been running on this terrain for a while and the ruts are deep, threatening to pull me in again. Now I'm in unfamiliar territory without a map. I don't want to screw things up and return to the well-walked path. I know those ruts lead to nowhere I want to go.

I remember feeling unsettled when I decided I needed to have better boundaries around working too many hours. I was used to completing my to-do list every day, regardless of how much time it took. But choosing to not complete everything made me feel like I was precariously close to something fatal. Of course that wasn't true, but it felt like something I highly valued was up for grabs—my productivity and even my sense of worthiness. I knew I needed to curb this habit and even die to getting my sense of worth from my level of productivity, but I wasn't entirely sure how to go about doing it. What was I to do about the things that wouldn't get done? How would I make choices about what work to leave and what work to finish? What would people think if I didn't deliver it to them like I had in the past? These are the questions of someone walking on a new path. But they are the right questions because they are being asked on the path of transformation.

Maybe you've had that experience too. You've curbed your spending habits, but know you're only one shopping trip away from falling back into old patterns. Perhaps you've truly forgiven your friend, but you're wary about getting hurt again. Or you've had new insight and closure with a family member, but a recent conversation is taking you off course. There are endless possibilities for rebirth:

You've been convicted by your habit of gossiping, but lately your insecurities are threatening to undo you. You've remained committed to your new approach but temptation feels like it's always close by. I get it. The early days of being reborn to something new can feel scary.

We've Got a Coach

In moments like these, I need to remind myself God isn't standing on the sidelines waiting impatiently for me to finally figure it out and get it all right. He isn't shaking his head in disgust, wondering why I haven't mastered all the plays. He's on the field with me. He's committed to coaching and equipping me the whole game through—not because he has to, but because he absolutely loves to. He knows I've mastered some plays. He's delighted in that progress and is wholeheartedly invested in the process of the ones I'm trying to master now.

He understands that being transformed into an "all-star player" doesn't happen overnight. He's not concerned when one day I get it right and the next day I don't. He knows that learning, rewiring and mastering new habits is a process. All he asks is that we stick with it and stick with him.

He can't work with people who are beating themselves up with guilt for not getting it right all the time, nor can he work with people who play the powerless victim. But he can work with someone who is daring enough to try and try again.

And, like any good coach, he knows there are many more new plays to learn down the road, ones we're not ready to take on quite yet. This is good news for those of us who feel like we should throw in the towel. If transformation is about me becoming the person God already sees me as, then I can be gentle with myself when I've not yet fully realized the change I long for.

Henri Nouwen explains it like this:

Jesus said, "Live ecstatically. Move out of that place of death and toward life because I am the God who is living. Wherever I am there is life, there is change, there is growth, there is increase and blossoming and something new. I am going to make everything new." For us to dare to live a life in which we continue to move out of the static places and take trusting steps in new directions—that is what faith is about. The Greek word for faith means to trust—to trust that the ground before you that you never walked on is safe ground, God's ground, holy ground.

Yes! Let's not run in static ruts but embrace something new and dynamic; the place where there is life.

Reformation is something to get giddy about! We've accepted the dare to walk through the valleys and shadows and now we're on the other side. We are witnesses to something brand new within us, and we know it's leading to better things. It's like the first crocus of spring poking through the snow, a sign we have the whole summer ahead of us. Or the clock on a Friday afternoon, signaling the start of weekend adventures. Rebirth is the finish line for death and the starting line for freedom and love.

On your marks. Get set. Go!

FREEDOM

"Tomorrow's freedom is today's surrender"
— *All Sons & Daughters*

Do you remember the last day of school before summer vacation? It's the last day you have to get up early to beat the first bell. It's the last day you have to make your lunch. It's the last day you have to sit and listen to your teacher. There were many years when I couldn't keep my eyes off the clock for the last forty-five minutes of that last day. I could hardly stand the wait. Those poor teachers didn't know what to do with themselves—they had all but lost control of the classroom. I bet they were counting down the seconds harder than any of us kids were.

When that final bell rang, we would storm out the doors as fast as our little legs could carry us. We could have beaten any Olympic speed-walker with our pace and most certainly with our determination. The final bell meant we would run out of those doors and not return for weeks and weeks and weeks. That bell meant that we could sleep in, play outside all day and eat lunches that hadn't gone soggy. It was pure, beautiful freedom.

Freedom is light. Freedom faces forward. Freedom makes you want to do the happy dance.

Folks, this is the best part! We've slogged through the challenges of surrender and feeling vulnerable. We've learned just how life-altering the process of transformation actually is—even to the point of dying to things we hold so dear. We've done the hard work of putting our bundles down to make room for something better. Freedom is the result of being made new. It's what we experience when we have been changed. When those musty, stale places in us have been renovated, we are free to experience more joy, peace and love.

Scripture is chock-full of examples of what freedom looks like. It reminds us that Jesus is the one who has the power to offer the freedom people long for. Remember, Jesus didn't experience death and rebirth to be transformed himself (he was already perfect). Jesus walked this way to usher in a new way for all of us.

Jesus healed groups of lepers from their painful and isolating disease so that they were freed up to live in the community with others. He healed blind men so they could finally see the beauty around them. A woman was healed of a blood disease, enabling her to live an active, fulfilling life. And a paralyzed man was brought by his friends to Jesus in the hopes he would be able to walk again. The freedom we crave comes from being healed of something that holds us back.

But Jesus didn't just heal physical problems. The freedom he brought reached into the deepest places of the human experience.

Mary was a woman shunned by her community and on the

brink of being stoned to death. Jesus offered her security, respect and dignity as a way to heal her shame and gave a way for her to move forward. She had been given a taste of what freedom looks like in the Kingdom of God.

Zacchaeus, a despised tax collector, was healed of his prideful and greedy ways. One profound lunchtime conversation with Jesus helped Zacchaeus see what was most important. He walked away from that meal knowing the Kingdom that Jesus talked about offered a far richer and more satisfying life than the Roman kingdom he had been serving.

Peter was also healed of his shame after denying his friendship with Jesus. When he was restored by Jesus' kind words of forgiveness, and was given a second chance to help lead Jesus' followers, Peter discovered that grace truly is life changing.

The Apostle Paul had an encounter with Jesus that changed everything for him, too. Paul was healed of his pride, arrogance and religious ways. Perhaps what had been fueling these things all along was fear. But Jesus came to Paul on that Damascus road and put these things to death. Paul was reborn and freed from the pious ways that stifled the connection with God he longed for. He was reborn to experience more of God's love, joy and peace.

Each of these people was in the position to receive something, even if they didn't know it. Like us, each of them longed to be loved, to feel secure and to know that they belonged. Most of them were aware of their need and, in their own way, surrendered themselves in an encounter with Jesus. They each had a sense of the things that held them back and the chains that held them captive. The freedom they dreamed about seemed unimaginable—and yet Jesus, in a way only he could, made their dreams come true. He gave them the treasure and they knew it was priceless. Peter, Paul, Zacchaeus, Mary, the blind and the lame were transformed, and as a result, the freedom they received pushed them straight into the arms of God.

Our freedom always leads to a greater dependence on God. That's the thing about transformation. We don't need to white-knuckle it in desperate hope that someday something might change. Instead, we can be rooted in the safe place where we are already accepted and where God is growing us and maturing us to experience more and more love.

Does this surprise you? Isn't the very nature of freedom an untethering from people and things?

Bound to the Beautiful

Let's take a closer look at what Scripture describes as the pinnacle of freedom. We've said before that we will all be in this constant journey of transformation until the end of days. But on that final day, our transformation will be complete and we will be completely free. The treasure will totally be ours. Scripture tells us on that day we are all invited to a wedding—our own wedding, in fact. This will be the day when all of creation will no longer need to groan for the freedom it longs for, and we will walk down the aisle towards our bridegroom—Jesus.

The Bible tells us the wedding feast will be the party of all parties! It will be an epic celebration where all God's children can finally rest with joy, complete security and wholeness. We'll be healed and free. Delectable food will be in abundance and wine will be overflowing for all the pilgrims to enjoy. Music, singing, smiles and laughter will rise to God in adoration and gratitude. There will be no more pain or decay. Death will have lost its sting for good. There will be no more grave. Sadness will never ever darken our door again—it will all have been swallowed up by Life. All the broken things will be made new. And everything will be saturated in perfect peace.

We will finally be together.

We will finally have come home.

We will finally be completely free.

Don't you think it's ironic that marriage is the image God uses to help us understand what true freedom will feel like? So many people feel trapped in their marriages. It's something from which they long to escape. That's tragic, really. So many people trade in their marriages for what they think will truly make them free.

And yet Scripture is clear right from the start: self-gratifying independence is not really freedom at all. When Adam and Eve decided to eat from the forbidden tree, they were not simply expressing their freedom to choose, but they were also walking away from relying on God. They thought their dependence on God limited their freedom. If only they had realized that their hearts longed to lean completely into God. The truest freedom we were designed to experience comes in intimate and organic friendship with God. Freedom is trusting that God is good, and depending on him to meet our needs. Freedom is radical dependence on God. This is the only way to experience the life that truly satisfies.

Does this feel like freedom to you? Does the idea of leaning fully on God for everything make you feel giddy like a kid running out the school door at the sound of the last bell? Or do you cringe because it feels suffocating and scary?

If you've ever met someone who lives with this type of faith and dependence on God, you have a sense of what it looks like. I know a few people. There is something genuine and non-threatening about them. They aren't trying to impress anyone and they have a peace that oozes out of their pores. They are comfortable in their own skin. Some would even say they look radiant. They have an authentic desire to serve God and seem to get into crazy situations that stretch them. Sure, they're not perfect nor are their life circumstances, but they've got a relationship with Jesus that seems to make a real difference in what they do, how they treat others and what they ultimately hope for. They are motivated by something far more significant than what the world offers. They make choices that seem strange by our culture's standards, but these very choices bring them a peculiar joy. Yes, these folks depend on God in such a way they actually seem excited about the adventures of the unknown. They live with a freedom that has been born out of struggle. They live as if the bell has rung and they are no longer trapped. They live knowing that everything they have and hope for is from God.

When God changes us, our willingness to engage in transformation becomes more about our desire for intimacy with him than simply about becoming a better person. We are freed up to live the way we were created to live. We drop the bundles of baggage we've been awkwardly carrying, and place our hands in God's. Like the caterpillar, we once were crawling around in the dirt, groping for what comforted us; now, in freedom, we're freely soaring to where God is leading. I'm not saying that we will experience absolute perfect freedom on this side of heaven, but I am saying that we can experience increasing degrees of abundance. As a bundle is put down, we become lighter. With each surrender, we become more free to walk closely with God.

Full Weight Down

I know where I've tasted this freedom in my own life. I know what it means to be in a process of being liberated from old ideas and habits that hold me back.

For many years I thought I was single because I was somehow defective. I wondered if something was inherently wrong with me because no one had chosen me. I was trapped in thoughts that had me struggling. I was drowning in insecurity, and doubted my beauty, femininity and loveliness. There was nothing freeing about these thoughts and feelings—the chains had me locked up tight.

After years and years of struggling, I started to surrender. I started to get brutally honest with how sad I was feeling. I began to acknowledge how lonely I felt instead of keeping busy with distractions. I began to ask God to help me when I felt unlovable. And perhaps the biggest surrender, the biggest vulnerability, the biggest death came when I faced the prospect of never marrying at all. It's here that I have had to ask myself some very tough questions: Do I actually believe God is good, has my best interests at heart and can be trusted? Seriously, can I actually trust him with my relationships or should I take matters into my own hands?

As I first began processing these questions, the thought of never getting married or having children felt like I would be shackled in the death zone for life. Like that Ann Weems poem I found after my brother died, I wondered if I would be *"left alone beneath a starless sky with a starless heart that barely beats."* There had never been a time in my life when I thought I wouldn't be married or have children. Surrendering to these questions was new territory and left me feeling unsettled, uncomfortable and even afraid.

Over the years, though, God has been transforming me. I've learned to embrace the vulnerability of my greatest fears. As I write this, I can see how God is slowly helping me change the old patterns of insecurity and self-sufficiency and inviting me to rely on him in new ways. Something new has been born in me because I have allowed something I've held on to so tightly to die. In truth, something new continues to be born and it's growing into something unexpectedly beautiful.

God is giving me a calm confidence to keep walking this way. My desire to get married isn't gone, but it's changed. It's not like I've turned into a marriage-hater and have gone all bitter. I've not sworn off marriage and I don't feel like I've been given the specific desire to be single for my whole life. I still feel all the vulnerability as I stay open to what God would have for me (marriage or not) and what path he wants me to follow him on.

But God is transforming my heart. The image of what my future will be like is less about the specifics (a husband, 2.5 kids, a dog and white picket fence), and more about the adventure of what God will do when I rest completely in him. I'm becoming less concerned about being "normal" (by being married) and more interested in embracing the courage and creativity that's required to live the life I have been given today. Don't get me wrong: I still have restless moments of doubt and longing, wondering if God actually knows what he's doing. I'm still a work in progress and wrestle to find where my needs for intimacy and companionship can be met. But as time passes, I'm finding more freedom in this area of my life. It's not making me more independent—it is pushing me closer and closer to my Father who knows my needs. I'm less concerned about the details of how I'll be cared for and more enamored with the journey.

Ironically, radical dependence on God feels like beautiful freedom.

One of the best pictures of freedom is found in a favorite movie of mine. I watched *The Fault in Our Stars* for the first time on a cross-Atlantic flight, and I was a total mess. I had to hold in my sobs and hide my face for fear that the people around me would think I'd had too much to drink.

I loved Augustus's explanation to Hazel Grace about why he pretends to smoke by keeping an unlit cigarette in his mouth. "You put the killing thing right between your teeth, but you don't give it the power to do its killing." Boom! That, in my estimation, is true freedom. It's when something that has the power to destroy you has been tamed and transformed and brings new power, perspective and life.

This is what God does with us. He doesn't just erase our lives and give us new ones; he takes our lives and changes them. Finding true freedom is not climbing the ladder out of our troubled lives—it's letting God climb down into those places. It's letting him have his way so that we finally discover that he can truly be trusted with the most delicate and sensitive parts of our lives.

God is in the business of transforming all the intricate, tricky places in us so that we can have beautifully free lives. Isolation and self-indulgence are ways we've coped in the past and it's never delivered the freedom we crave. But God knows a better way. He wants to lead us on an adventure to find the treasure. He dares us to lean our full weight on him, knowing that when we do, we'll taste the sweetness of freedom.

So let's go! The bell has rung. Freedom is ours! Let's bolt for the doors, fling them wide open and run fast into the adventure of following where God leads!

LOVE

"If sympathy for the world's wounds is not enlarged by our anguish,
if love for those around us is not expanded,
if gratitude for what is good does not flame up,
if insight is not deepened,
if commitment to what is important is not strengthened,
if aching for a new day is not intensified,
if hope is weakened and faith diminished,
if from the experience of death comes nothing
good, then death has won."
— *Nicholas Wolterstorff*

I've been practicing yoga on and off for a few years now, and every so often between a downward facing dog, an eagle, or a tree pose, yoga offers me a glimpse of how we're all connected.

Normally in class, I'm in the zone. Don't talk to me. Don't look at me. Stay in your own space. In fact, I do my darnedest to try and shut out everything and everyone with the exception of the teacher's instructions.

But every so often, when a pose is particularly difficult, one by one people start to sweat, shake, breathe heavier and clumsily fall out of the pose, chuckling to themselves. I'm usually one of them.

It's in those moments that I catch someone's eye and we smile knowingly to each other, a little bashful that we're no longer striking the beautiful pose. I'm reminded that I'm not in this on my own. I'm surrounded by people who are on the same human journey of struggle and the pursuit of freedom as me.

My yoga studio's logo is a butterfly and its slogan is: "Transform yourself, transform your work, transform the world around you." They're on to something here. This adage points to something greater than us. We don't embark on the transformation journey for transformation's sake, but for something bigger and more important. We participate and welcome life change so that we are freed up to love and change the world. While I think the yoga studio is far too optimistic and hopeful in people's individual ability to truly change themselves from the inside out, I still appreciate that we're all chasing the same thing. The whole world desperately needs to be reformed, and God puts us in the center of his plan to do just that.

You and I are not transformed so that we can experience freedom from our old ways. No, we are freed up from our old ways so that we can love better. You can't jump from rebirth directly to love because we can only love well when we have experienced the freedom that comes from being loved ourselves.

Freedom means the chains have fallen off and we're able to live closer with God, depending on him and experiencing more of his love. And when we experience this love, we are able to give more generously, love more liberally, care more creatively and better companion others with mercy and love. God's love transforms us and always leads to more love.

The Means to the End

Think of it this way. You don't earn your salary so that you can have lots of money stored away in your bank account. You earn your salary so that you can freely make withdrawals from the account and use the money to make purchases. You don't go grocery shopping so that you can have full cupboards rather than empty ones. You shop so that you will be able to pull food from your cupboards to prepare things to eat. You don't go to university so that you can acquire knowledge that stays in your brain; you go to school and learn things so that you'll have some freedom as you make choices about your future. There is a larger purpose to earning money, going grocery shopping and getting a degree. Transformation is like that too.

The purpose of our transformation is not to simply experience freedom. When old habits and attitudes die, those broken, fractured parts in us are mended and made more whole. In this way we are becoming more like Jesus, and in this freedom, we participate with him in his mission to make all things new.

How can regular people with regular issues change the world? What could happen if we all decided to submit ourselves to God and experience personal transformation in very specific areas in our lives? Let's see what it might look like.

I am friends with a man named "Bill". When he was a kid, Bill's parents often told him he was stupid. As a result, insecurity haunted him throughout his life. He consistently spent his money on things that would numb the painful emotional wound he carried. He would buy new clothes and personal trinkets to compensate for feeling poorly about himself. Being well-dressed with lots of man-toys helped him to feel he was worth something.

Over time, Bill became more and more aware of his need to get some sort of healing in this area of his life. When he quieted himself long enough to be close to God, this need popped up on the radar every time. It came up more and more often in conversations with his girlfriend, and it seemed like everything he was reading and listening to had something that caught his attention in this area.

Bill became open to having God do some work in him. He spent time praying about it. He decided to go to a counselor for a few sessions. He faced the tough sting of emotions as he processed some of his childhood memories. Over time, he realized he needed to die to the idea that money would bring him the satisfaction he was really looking for. He had to become aware of his impulse to purchase new things when he was feeling particularly vulnerable.

If you asked Bill how he feels today, he'd explain that over time those painful parts of his childhood had less and less power over him. As a result, he felt *more* free to spend *less* money on himself, and instead to give it away to others who needed it more than he did. Bill isn't carrying that bundle of shame any longer. God has birthed something new in him and as a result, he is able to participate in God's mission to bring aid and care to others in some pretty significant ways.

Do you see how being transformed in an area in our lives actually can make a difference for others in the world? Author and contemplative activist Phileena Heuertz reminds us that "To the degree that we are transformed, the world is transformed." Bill is changing the world because God changed him.

Or take "Julia" for example. Julia is married with three kids and has a pretty great life. Her husband is attentive and the kids are thriving in their schools. But there was something that nagged at Julia every time she looked in the mirror. You see, before she had her kids, Julia was a busy executive climbing the ladder of success. While she didn't regret the decision to stay at home and take care of her family, she constantly wondered if she was living a significant life anymore. She got frustrated and jealous quickly, and when conversations among her friends turned to celebrating different accomplishments, she shut down. She wished she could engage but no matter how hard she tried, she felt envious and withdrawn. Her relationships were getting weaker and she felt like she was living in the shallows.

Like Bill, Julia knew this was something she needed Jesus to help her with. She had lots of hard conversations where she invited feedback from friends. She meditated on specific Scripture passages that talked about what her true significance was and she spent a number of months asking others to forgive her for how she had been acting. She was swimming in vulnerability but it was paying off. Slowly over time, she realized she didn't feel threatened by those around her getting promotions or receiving accolades. She even started to enjoy celebrating others' accomplishments. Instead of withdrawing, she was able to enter into deeper friendship with people, sharing not only in their celebrations but also walking alongside them when things took a turn.

Julia is now a friend people reach out to in times of trouble. She's exactly where she wants to be. She finds freedom and significance in all the right places. She's changing the world.

And finally, there's "Susan" who loved to work. She was good at it and her colleagues affirmed her. Every place Susan was employed, she was told she was incredibly productive. It would be normal for Susan to work long hours because she loved her job; it never really felt like a burden. However, over the course of many years, Susan found it difficult to think about anything but work. It got to the point where she worked so hard that the weekends got shorter and shorter, and any time left was simply spent recovering from the pace of the week. There was no time for anything else. Eventually Susan realized something had to change.

In quiet times of prayer, Susan began to see that her compulsion to work was more about pushing back on the loneliness she felt. Those long hours of intense work acted as a refuge and helped her feel secure. Yet, she was tired of carrying this load. Her world had collapsed down to a single focus and the color was draining from her life.

As Susan surrendered to the transformation that Jesus was inviting her to enter, she faced the regret of the many moments in the past few years she had lost to her work. She started learning how to reach out so she wouldn't feel so alone, and worked hard to have the discipline to stop working extra hours. She died to the idea that she was a mini-god who had control over all of her work, and she started to learn how to rest and be refreshed on a regular basis. She began to trust she was still worthy, even if the work wasn't all done.

Now, Susan has much more time to enjoy life and give to others. She volunteers at the local seniors' home and is trying to make friends with those who would otherwise be forgotten. Her sense of security is no longer tied to her productivity. She has more margins to simply enjoy life, and the gratitude she feels spills out onto others.

Do you see how being transformed in one area in our lives actually makes a difference for others in the world? I know I do, because "Susan" is me. This is a transformation I've experienced over the past few years. Do I still need to grapple with the temptation to use work to compensate for loneliness? Yes! But I have come a long way and the life change I've experienced has led to more love—love for God, love for myself and love for others.

When you take a closer look at Julia, Bill and Susan's stories, you can identify all eight themes of transformation. If we want to inhale a full, high-definition life of love then we need to exhale what has gone stale and monochromatic, and is holding us back. As we remain open and surrender to transformation, God maneuvers like a surgeon does, cutting away parts with a loving precision so that we can heal and live lives of love.

A lifestyle of abundance looks like gratitude, rest, simplicity, peace, beauty, generosity and compassion. Poet William Blake reminds us that "We are put on earth for a little space that we might learn to bear the beams of love". This "surgery" enables us to bear these beams of love with greater brilliance and light.

Change the World—Really?

You and I both know the world is pretty messed up and in desperate need of renovation. I'm not about to chime off a bunch of statistics about global poverty. The number of children that will die from preventable diseases on this very day is too high. Millions of people still drink dirty water full of bacteria because there are no clean sources to access. There are fathers around the globe who are unable to earn enough money to buy food for their families, and mothers who put their crying, hungry children to bed night after night. There are countless little girls unable to receive an education. They struggle to make a way for themselves and are left to take a tragic path that leads to nowhere. Millions are fleeing the nightmare of war and leaving everything they know and have just to survive another day of hell on earth.

And there is so much pain and struggle right in our own backyards. People are overextended, lonely and depressed more than ever. Thousands still find themselves sleeping on the streets in the bitter cold of winter. Children go to school hungry, while minority groups struggle to rise above stigmas. No, you and I don't need the stats to know that something is very broken. We are certainly aware of all of these things. Our awareness must lead to action, and this action must look like love.

There's a colossal mess of hurt, abuse, poverty and pain on the planet. How on earth are we able to make a real difference? Shouldn't we leave saving the world up to someone with a cape and superpowers? How does our personal transformation really make a dent in something like this?

The truth is that God's Plan A is to show his love and care for the world through you and me. His game-day strategy is for us to share the love we've received with others. You could say we are transformed so we can transform others. The church I used to work at had this guiding principle: "We are a transforming community that transforms communities." It's crazy and inspiring. It's simple but not easy.

Henri Nouwen explains it like this: "As you love deeply, the ground of your heart will be broken more and more, but you will rejoice in the abundance of the fruit it will bear." We are made to love and be loved. It's the Kingdom economy of abundance. Love begets more love begets more love.

Remember the equation of transformation? Something must die for a new thing to be born.

When selfishness dies, generosity is born.

When anxiety dies, peace emerges.

When pride dies, compassion flourishes.

When perfection dies, we realize we are enough.

When addiction dies, there is more room for love.

When fear dies, joy is born.

Don't you think healing the world will come through things like generosity, peace and compassion? I do. Imagine the difference more of our love and joy could make in the darkest places on our planet. I'm not sure there is any better motivation to embrace our own transformation than this. It's a brilliant, beautiful exchange!

What Could Love Look Like?

There's a place in rural Zambia called "The Fires" that is etched into my heart forever.

The sun was just about to start its descent for the day and leave behind a golden glow that would live up to its "magic hour" reputation. Soon the sky would match the hue of the red, dusty earth. Standing behind a wire fence that separates the hospital compound from the community, I was glued to the scene in front of me. Dozens and dozens of people, mostly women and children, were gathered in small circles around their tiny cooking fires, preparing for the evening meal and the long dark night ahead. The small streams of smoke would rise, carrying flakes of ash and the smell of charcoal. Soon, the only thing I'd see would be a throng of tiny orange flickers of fire, dancing among the shadows, scattered across the field.

Why were these people here? Why had they made the long journey by foot to the hospital some twenty, thirty, forty kilometers away? These people huddled over their fires were friends and family members of patients staying inside the hospital and they had made their temporary home there to stand vigil with them. These people companioned their loved ones to the hospital, set up their makeshift homes and committed to visit their loved ones in the hospital, often bringing them their meals.

I couldn't believe what I was witnessing. This was what dedication and commitment looked like. This was what sacrifice and solidarity sounded like. This was what compassion and love smelled like.

What could love look like? The people at The Fires had their own answer to that question. Their sacrifice rose with the smoke of their fires as a beautiful fragrant offering to God. When we are freed up to love, we are not bound by our own rights and privileges. We are not driven by ease and convenience. No, when we are free, love looks like generosity, sacrifice and compassion.

So, what could love look like for us? How might the new freedom you and I have found impact our relationships? Does our freedom lead us to new areas of interest? Has our relationship with money, power or even our ego been altered so that we can give more of ourselves away in service to others? The more God does his work in us, the more we are able to give our love away.

Don't we all love to love?

The Apostle Paul spends a great deal of time addressing transformation and the freedom that God gives. It's as if he is begging the readers of his letters to understand that God's love, experienced through personal transformation, is the only thing that can compel them to love others. He can't help himself. He had experienced a radical transformation himself and was filled with this love. He understood how compelling God's love was—it was his sole motivation to reach out and serve others.

Are you and I compelled to love others out of this new freedom we've been given? I know my natural tendency is to protect and preserve myself at the expense of others. And God knows it too. I need to pay close attention to figuring out what my love will tangibly look like, cling closely to God and respond—otherwise I'll drift. It's not okay unless I give it away.

Here are five questions we can ask ourselves to help us get super-specific about what love could look like this year:

- Who are the people around me who are lonely? How can I give more love to them?

- How am I using my resources (time, money, talents and influence) to love others? Is God nudging me to give more of my resources to others?

- Who are the marginalized and vulnerable in my city who could benefit from my tangible expression of love? What's my next step?

- Who are the marginalized and vulnerable around the world who could benefit from my tangible expression of love? What's my next step?

- How can the people closest to me experience more of my love this year?

The Powerful First Step

What would happen if you answered and responded in action to just one of those questions? Imagine if everyone who read this page did that. Imagine if we all took seriously for a moment that we have been given the privilege and the responsibility to get ruthless about living lives of love. What if we all took one concrete step today? Our first step towards showing our love may seem inconsequential in the grand scheme of things, but never underestimate the power of the first step. I believe that when we take consistent faithful steps to give love to others, we can change the world.

In many ways, we are back to where we started. The more we share our love and serve others, the more we are transformed. Transformation is cyclical and never ends on this side of heaven. I wholeheartedly agree with Bob Goff when he explains, "I imagine God sees who I'll become as I start RSVPing 'yes' to His invitations and go after those things He's made us to love. It's not all planned out for us either, and that's where most people get too nervous to take the next step. But know this, when Jesus invites us on an adventure, He shapes who we become with what happens along the way." As I share my love in tangible ways, I end up opening myself to learning more about others. And with each step, I surrender to the vulnerability of what this new relationship will require of me. It has all the potential of birthing something new in me—something that will likely look like love!

Love. It's the essence of the universe. It's the oxygen we breathe, the waters we swim in, the music we hear. It heals and resurrects. Love is a force greater than any other and has the power to change everything. It is in front and behind, within and all around us. It saturates and it overwhelms.

Love is who God is, not just what he does.

Love is a mystery worth embracing.

Love is a gift to be received, and a gift to be given away.

ULTREÏA!

Ultreïa: The word Ultreïa has the meaning of "onward" or "keep going", and is used as an encouragement to pilgrims on the way to the shrine of St. James at Santiago de Compostela in northwest Spain.

KEEP GOING!

*"The mystery of human existence lies not in just staying
alive, but in finding something to live for."*
— *Fyodor Dostoyevsky*

There I was, before sunrise, crying on a bench somewhere in Spain.
I was huddled over my knees trying to put on my hiking boots.
And I was wondering if I could take another step.

That summer, I had the blissful opportunity to hike the Camino
de Santiago, an eight-hundred kilometer solo trek through north-
ern Spain. I struck out on my own, desperate to discover something that would change me, and hoping this ancient pilgrimage
path would deliver. I'm not sure I even knew what I was searching
for but I went to Spain to find it. That bench in the early morning
dark was the birthplace for that something I had been looking for.

The Camino is an incredible place and has been traveled by
millions since as early as the tenth century. Pilgrims (as they are
called) travel over mountains, across rivers, through vineyards

and small, remote villages towards their final destination, the city of Santiago de Compostela. Ancient pilgrims from medieval times would start their journey in their hometowns all over Europe, traveling through hostile territory with only the clothes on their back. They would risk their lives in order to travel to their final destination. There was never any guarantee they would arrive safe and well in Santiago.

On my very first night on the Camino, after having walked eight hours over the Pyrenees mountains, I was having dinner with other pilgrims who had just completed the same stretch. We had all begun that morning, each of us not entirely sure how the next eight hundred kilometers would go. Our conversation was peppered with details about our lives back home, how we had experienced the brutal uphill climbs and breathtaking vistas of the day, and what we were hoping to experience over our journey. We were like little puppies, excited with everything around us, never able to keep our attention on any one conversation for very long. We were also blissfully ignorant of the struggle we'd face in the month to come, and the dramatic change our lives would undergo because of our pilgrimage.

Our conversation turned to the history of the pilgrimage. Adrian, a student from Austria who was an armchair historian, explained to us that ancient pilgrims had a greeting for one another on the path. "Ultreïa! Ultreïa!" they would say as they met up with other pilgrims. The expression is Latin, meaning "Keep going! Onward and upward!" The greeting was intended to encourage weary pilgrims who were wondering if they could actually take another step. When Adrian described this, I was mesmerized. I could actually hear a voice within me say, "Pay attention to this— it's important." I took out my book and made a note of it, not even sure how to spell it.

Over the course of the next thirty-one full days of walking, I began to understand why "Ultreïa!" was exactly the right message to hold in my heart. It was the nugget of power I needed when my feet were swollen and too tender to stand on. It was the precious message of persuasion coaxing me to get out of my chair when all I wanted to do was rest. It was the whisper from deep within that got me off the bench in those early morning hours, helped me brush my tears aside and walk out alone into the dark, Spanish countryside. "Keep going. Just take a few more steps," was my mantra when the road felt too long.

I don't think any of us sitting around that table eating crusty bread and spicy chorizo soup—or the millions of pilgrims who started the journey before us—could have known how often we would be reminded of that ancient pilgrim greeting of encouragement. To my surprise, I saw this word everywhere: spray-painted on bridges, written on rocks, displayed on signs. Every time I saw this word, it was as if a host of cheerleaders were bearing witness to my struggle. Someone somewhere knew this journey was hard, and wanted me to know I wasn't alone.

The entire Camino experience is full of metaphors for the spiritual life—far too many to capture here. But this greeting—" Ultreïa!"—is important for us as we wrap up our conversation about transformation.

What does it mean to keep going as we dare to risk it all and embrace God's life change in us? What does it mean to keep taking steps towards the abundant life God is creating within and around us? How do we keep going when we're too weary to take another step?

In order to keep going, we need to hold onto a few lifelines that will help us on this path. We need to:

Seek the sweet.

Lean on others.

Hold the long view.

Keep going friends! We can do this.

13

SEEK THE SWEET

"For the grateful person knows that God is good, not by hearsay but by experience. And that is what makes all the difference."
— *Thomas Merton*

I have a unique relationship with berries. It's strange, I know. Fresh local berries are my favorite food. Tied for a close second are cheese, chocolate and any kind of warm bread.

Blueberries, strawberries, blackberries, raspberries, Saskatoon berries—you name it, I love them all. Some of my most vivid food memories are of eating berries. The fresh strawberry pie devoured on the boat in mid-June—it was like we welcomed summer with that pie. Or the wild blueberries handpicked way up north with friends; we picked those berries wondering if we'd run into a bear. Afterwards my friend made sweet, thick jam so we could take some home. Or the wild raspberries that fed me on the trail in Spain; they always seemed to turn up when I needed a boost.

Perhaps the most vivid memory of all is of testing a local farmer's blackberries at the summer market in South Haven, Michigan. My friend and I took a bite of those berries and were stopped in our tracks, just staring at each other with wide-eyed delight. We couldn't believe how big and juicy those black jewels were. We bought a few pints on the spot and told every passerby to do the same. The farmer actually asked if I was looking for a commission.

Biting into a sweet berry is a foodie game changer. Of course, the risk is there to bite into a sour one, but when you've sunk your teeth into a sweet morsel, you feel like you've won the lottery. Time stops for a second. The quest to find the sweet ones intensifies and you savor every one because you know the berry season is always too short.

We've been doing a lot of talking about the pain and challenge transformation requires. There's no doubt this is true in so many cases. We don't really like to change and so the energy we must muster to partner with God in being transformed can be hard. Some of the stuff that's changed us the most has been really painful. But I don't want us to neglect the ways the sweet seasons in our lives change us too. If we want to keep going as pilgrims on this journey, we have to seek out the sweet moments.

Great moments strung together make a season of some really good stuff. There is still a surrender and vulnerability—even a death of sorts in seasons like these—but really good things can be the grace-filled way God changes us as well. If we want to keep going and continue to submit to being changed, then we need to realize God is using all the good stuff to show us his abundance as much as he does the hard stuff. Let me show you what I mean.

Think, for example, about the new job promotion you got. Sure, you've got more responsibility and a different team, and the job requires something new of you. If you're going to rise to the challenge, you need to surrender yourself to the new role, open yourself up to vulnerability and even "die" to some old work habits. But it's a perfect fit. You've grown more confident in yourself, you're using your gifts and helping more people. You've never been happier. You experience a new freedom within yourself as new skills and work routines are born, and as a result you are able to give more of yourself away to others. You've been transformed by a sweet season of life.

Or maybe you've just had your first child. There's no question you've had to surrender to parenthood and feel the fragility of that place. You've had to die to your life without children— surely something to grieve. But there has literally and figuratively been a birth and it's changed everything. You had no idea you could love like this. You're more in love with life and more hopeful for the future. You're closer to God, and for the first time in a long time, you feel at peace. Love has been born. Yes, this is certainly a sweet season.

Maybe you've fallen in love with someone and you're finding the old, unhealthy ways of thinking about yourself are being replaced by confidence. Where you were once insecure, you're now more comfortable. You are starting to believe you really are special and lovely. You've surrendered to the vulnerability that comes with being in a relationship and your single life has been put to death so to speak. Moment after moment, love is growing.

Yes, transformation can happen in the sweet seasons of life. Those sweet moments, strung together in joy, are a beautiful place we can experience God changing us.

Taking Notice

Monk and priest Thomas Keating once said, "God will bring people and events into our lives, and whatever we may think about them, they are designed for the evolution of His life in us." I think I've spent too much time assuming God only transforms me through the hard stuff. That somehow I have to battle through everything in order to become more mature. When I read that Keating quote in the past, my mind would go directly to the difficult events, never to the good ones. I thought the rate and level of transformation in my life was directly correlated to how painful it was. But that's just not true. God heals and continues to make me whole through the beautiful and sweet things.

So this gets me to thinking: What are the sweet and beautiful things God is bringing into my life that are really changing me? What good stuff is making me more like him? If I just focus on the sour, bitter things as evidence of God working in me, I'm going to get pretty tired of it all. Before long, I'm likely to throw my hands up in the air and quit. I've got to keep my eye out for the sweet.

If God is in fact using the sweet moments to transform me as much as the difficult ones, then I want to take notice. I want to look for him in the lovely. Barbara Brown Taylor writes in *An Altar in the World*, "The exercise of reverence generally includes knowing your rank in the overall scheme of things. It's the proper attitude of a small and curious human being in a vast and fascinating world of experience. Full appreciation of it required frequent adventures, grand projects, honed skills, and feats of daring." The sweet seasons in our lives are made sweeter when we revere them. A good day becomes a great day when we are full of gratitude for it. The best way to savor the sweet is to admire it, not let it pass by. We can make time stop for a second by pouring our awe and thankfulness to the Giver.

If I'm serious about my transformation, then I need to be a

curator of the sweet moments and ask myself how these moments strung together actually change me. Could the very act of reverence for God align me more with the abundant life he's offering me? I think so. I love how Allison Vesterfelt puts it: "As long as you're a spectator in your life, you're not a worshipper of God."

As I bear witness to the beauty, elegance and harmony in life, I testify to the grandeur, goodness and deep love of God. I worry less and pray more. I exhale anxiety to make room to breathe in peace. When I take notice and am in awe of the good, I feel dwarfed by beauty and I know my place. I recognize God as the One who creates and holds it all. He creates, recreates and holds me, too. When I seek the sweet, I find that everything else falls into place.

So where's the risk involved in this? One could argue this doesn't feel like daring at all.

But I disagree. Sometimes the bravest thing we can do is to take our eyes off ourselves and look for God in the seemingly mundane. Stopping long enough from our to-do lists to intentionally acknowledge the presence of God in the ordinary can be a radical act. Can we do this when we are overworked and exhausted? No. Can we do this sitting in front of the TV, or absorbing another season of Netflix? Maybe, but not likely. Are we able to take notice in our busy, isolated, lives? Doubtful. Noticing sweet moments is taking a step away from activities that numb and weary us, and this is truly a courageous act. Seeking God takes focus and a quiet heart. Being struck in awe requires margins. If they are too thin, crowded out by worry, busyness and fatigue, we just don't have the reserves to notice. Our ability to feel God's love has to do with the ability to savor all the gifts he gives.

I need to remind myself to go for a walk instead of watching television. To spend the hour preparing a delicious meal instead of ordering cardboard take out. To sit quietly for fifteen minutes and breathe instead of playing a game on my phone or reviewing my to-do list. The truth is that in order to notice the sweet morsels in our lives, we need to slow down, take time and actually pick them as we do berries. Hold them. Smell them. Taste them. This is a path that will certainly lead to a vibrant, satisfying life.

I've found the sweetest tasting berries of all are the ones I pick myself. Even though they may not technically blow the sweet-o-meter off the chart, they still taste best. I think it's in the effort and the up-close-ness of it all. The out-of-season, artificially bloated, cardboard-y berries, glowing on the shelves of the sterile super-market are not the stuff of awe. But taking your basket into the field on a hot June morning just after the dew has burned off, bending over small plants or thumbing through the dirt in search for ruby red gifts—this is abundance. We can find the sweet when we give the moment time, engage all our senses, get in touch with our smallness and search for the One who is bigger than ourselves.

So whether it is a great promotion or new love, strawberries or sunsets, a great song or a kind word from a friend, the sweetness of life points to love and the giver of those nuggets of goodness. The more we notice, standing in reverence, the sweeter it all becomes. And this undeniably transforms us and ushers an abundance of life.

WE'RE IN THIS TOGETHER

*"Kinship is a rich bondedness that calls forth to
the deepest parts of ourselves.
It is a mutuality of understanding,
a sense of belonging, a union of spirits,
a loving appreciation, and a deep communion
which comes from having known experiences similar to
the person with whom we are bonded."*
— Joyce Rupp

I have something embarrassing to admit: when I was a kid, I had cement statues for friends. Pathetic, right? I know.

When I was seven years old there were no kids in my small town to play with. Seriously, there were only five people in my second grade class. We all sat in one row right by the teacher's desk—tallest in the back, shortest in the front. Brad sat at the back, Ted in the front and three of us girls switched a few times during the year depending on who was growing the fastest and who was chatting too much to Brad. Actually, Brad did live in town, but he was a boy, so that didn't count.

Summer holidays sometimes felt too long. If my brother was playing baseball or biking with his friends, I'd be left to amuse myself. Just next door to our house was a small garden center where flowers, plants and all things lawn-care were sold. Out front there was a tiny tribe of lawn ornaments from small dwarfs to a family of deer. There was one very large, very animated-looking white horse that I named "Whitey". (Very creative. I know.) I'd stroll down the sidewalk by my house and sit and talk with these statues until I got bored with the very one-sided conversation we were having.

It does seem pitiful when I think about it now, but it doesn't matter what age we are, we crave companionship. We're hard-wired for it. I outgrew my stone friends pretty quickly but the fact that I befriended them at all reminds me I am created to be known and loved, to belong and to bond with others. If we want to keep going on this journey of transformation, we need to acknowledge our need—the need to lean on others.

God seems to prefer birthing something new in us when we have the support of others, not in isolation.

He nudges people to prompt us to be open to change.

He gives us examples of other people who have bravely surrendered to the things that frighten them most.

He provides people who encourage us when we feel most vulnerable.

He places people in our lives to hold out hope when we are discouraged.

He speaks through people, reminding us who we really are and who we are becoming.

He uses others to help hold out the vision of freedom when we need it most.

He surrounds us with people who can celebrate this new life as we begin to embrace it.

God tangibly shows us his love through the love we receive from others. And those people who show us love fuel our transformation.

He uses family, friends and sometimes strangers in every aspect of our transformation.

When I was walking the Camino, there were countless times I needed to lean on others. Whether it was asking for directions, getting a bag of ice for my shin, having a woman tape my ankle or getting advice on where to spend the night, I needed their help. And others leaned on me, too. I shared my water and sometimes bought a meal for another traveler. I listened to people's stories and celebrated with them when we all arrived at our hostel each night. The journey was only possible and made more meaningful because of my connection with fellow pilgrims.

Here's another simple example of the importance of friendship.

As I was in the process of writing this very chapter, two guys I work with suggested we get together and catch up. At the end of our conversation, in the middle of a coffee shop, they prayed for me. I wasn't expecting it from them, but it was exactly what I needed. They thanked God for what he had done in my life. They asked that I would be given strength and wisdom as I wrote this book. I don't think they had any idea just how important that moment was for me. I had been really struggling, and the very specific words they used while praying for me were ones that spoke into my insecurities, reminding me I wasn't alone. God used my two friends to show his love for me in the most perfect way. I left our conversation feeling renewed and encouraged. I was reminded that I wasn't really doing this on my own. That small moment helped me take my next step.

Connection with other people is powerful, and having solid spiritual communities supporting us is essential to our transformation—not optional or optimal, but essential.

Dysfunction Junction

The cringe factor is high when it comes to really sharing ourselves with others, I know. I can hear you now, "Why would I want to share some of my most vulnerable parts with others? People are crazy. They've got their own baggage. How can I trust someone with this stuff?" I'm often tempted to think it would be a whole lot easier if we could walk this journey of transformation on our own. But it's not the way God set it up. The fullness of transformation comes through the support, care, wisdom and counsel of others.

The entire story of Scripture is pregnant with images and stories about people living in community with one another. Adam didn't want to be alone. He desired intimacy and companionship with another and God gave him Eve. God sent the nation of Israel on a journey to freedom together as a chosen people. The disciples learned who they really were as followers of Jesus together, not alone. Paul wrote letters that addressed communities of believers, not just a person here and another there. The image of heaven is that of a festive wedding party, not a lonesome gathering of one. You can't read Scripture without getting a sense for just how highly God deems it necessary for us to be connected and in relationship with one another.

Here's the tricky thing: we have to be willing and open to inviting others in. Spiritual friendship, like any relationship, takes effort and a willingness to engage. We have to risk sharing our stories with others; even risk the possibility they won't care. We have to open up and share those private places, knowing someone just might not get it. We have to be willing to listen and walk alongside folks who are struggling. We have to take a chance on people, work to build our teams and extend grace to others when they don't always get it right.

Many of us have trouble trusting people, or we expect too much from them. Perhaps you have been really hurt and let down in the past. Maybe you feel like you don't know how to connect well with others. Many of us feel like we've been looking for a long time, and there just doesn't seem to be any safe kindred spirits around to share life with. I know it can be hard.

Here are a few questions we can ask ourselves: Who is in my life right now that I am open with? What makes them feel safe? In what ways do I try to control who I share my life with and how much I share? Why do I do this? What steps could I take to "die" to some of my control and instead let myself feel the vulnerability that comes with sharing more of my life with someone? As I talk to God about these things, who comes to mind? Do I need to take a risk and have a conversation with someone about how I'm feeling?

If you already belong to a church, it's quite possible you organize yourselves into small groups to give you the most optimal opportunity to experience this type of spiritual community. Often, the bar is high and idyllic for these groups—they are to be places where we love one another, learn and serve together, and find our sense of belonging in a spiritual family. In the best case scenarios, these groups are where we can find a couple of people to dive into the important stuff. Psychiatrist and author M. Scott Peck says, "There can be no vulnerability without risk; and there can be no community without vulnerability; and there can be no peace—ultimately no life—without community." It's a pretty sweet deal when it works well and it's worth the effort to go after.

But spiritual family—like any family—is messy. It's an inclusive experience and this means there will be people who don't feel like your tribe right away. In your group, there could be a person who's like your crazy uncle who never knows when enough is enough. Or the annoying woman who's like your sister and can't seem to keep it zipped long enough for you to get a word in edgewise. Then there's the person who's like that cousin you don't seem to understand—a different breed altogether. The leaders might be a bit weak, the group might be a needy lot and you're not sure if you should hitch your wagon to them. Just because it is a spiritual family does not mean it is dysfunction-free! But do you know what? It is still better than going it alone. You may need to shop around until you find a few people or a small group that feels like a good fit, but when you do, you are in the zone for God to move and change you through others. And he will use you to change them.

Weary pilgrims need something more than willpower to keep going. As we walk the path of transformation, let's find some friends and do it together. Let's take notice along the way and look for God in the beautiful and the sweet. Let's remember that many have gone before us and have discovered the way to the treasure is always found by taking just one more step.

15

HOLD THE LONG VIEW

"Waiting time is not wasting time.
Waiting patiently in expectation is the foundation
of the spiritual life."
— Henri Nouwen

When I was walking in Spain, there were a few moments I wondered if I'd actually make it to the end. Apparently it takes the average Camino pilgrim about a million steps to walk all those miles. Whether it was the thousandth, hundred-thousandth or five-hundred-thousandth step, I had to keep my eye on that western horizon in hopes of one day taking my last step in front of the cathedral in Santiago. I needed to keep the long view in mind, the end goal of my journey while I took every step—especially when I found the steps almost impossible to take.

When I was out of breath on a steep uphill climb, I had to hold that vision closely in my heart. When my feet screamed in agony, I had to remember that my arrival in Santiago would be the culmination of my struggle. I would finally stop walking. Standing in the old square in front of the cathedral would usher in the end of any pain, and be a catalyst for the joy of completing my long, long walk. I had to keep the long view in mind while I waited for my journey to be complete.

The Wait

I don't know anyone who likes to wait. Waiting always seems to have a negative feel to it, doesn't it? I remember waiting to be reunited with friends during the summer between my freshman and sophomore years in college. It was excruciating. Every day felt like time passed by more and more slowly. I pined for that first day back on campus, thinking it would never come. Every moment was filled with agitation. I was a miserable mess.

We wait for lots of things, don't we? We wait for buses to come, we often worry as we wait in doctors' aptly named waiting rooms and we wait for dinners to be served. By very definition, waiting means that you're delaying an action until a particular time in the future or until something else happens. It's this in-between time that often feels void of purpose. Waiting is the place where hope often wanes, endurance fades and patience withers.

Anticipating something or expecting an event is very much like waiting, except it has a much more positive vibe to it. We expect babies to arrive and anticipate seeing old friends. I anticipate my vacation in the sunny south and I eagerly await the party on Saturday night. Anticipation still occurs between two events, but there's something inherently satisfying and energizing about it. Anticipation can strengthen faith, leaving courage intact and devotion unbroken.

The transformation process is full of these "in-the-meantime" moments—moments where the change we desire feels far off if not impossible altogether. The trick is to frame these moments correctly, to rise above the feelings of discouragement, frustration and sadness, and to see the bigger picture of what's really going on.

Sue Monk Kidd, American author, says it like this: "Waiting... it means struggling with the vision of who we really are in God and molding the courage to live that vision." We can choose to endure the process by waiting in agitation and despair, or we can prevail with courage and devotion, seeing things with the eyes of faith that anticipate transformation.

I often wish my life could change by eliminating my current story completely and starting over with a brand spanking new one. Sometimes there are parts of me that would love a complete do-over. But that's not how it works. Transformation happens when we embrace the story we are already in rather than wishing it away. We're invited to experience it all in real-time, even the uphill and painful moments, and at the same time anticipate that every single thing will be redeemed from broken to beautiful—step by step by step.

Ache and struggle are as true a reality as the freedom and love of transformation we've been talking about. How do we reconcile these two competing realities? Maybe you're asking yourself the same sorts of questions I am. What happens when I accept the dare and make myself vulnerable, but it just doesn't work out? What happens if I risk it all but don't experience the freedom and love I long for? How can I keep taking risks and open myself up to vulnerability if I just keep getting hurt?

Maybe it plays out something like this:

You've tried for every promotion that comes up but you never seem to get it.

Your spouse has been stuck in that rut for so long and you're starting to fall out of love.

You've tried to lose the weight for as long as you can remember.

Your relationship with your parents is perpetually rocky despite your attempts to fix it.

You've seen too much devastation and injustice and you wonder if it's some cruel cosmic joke.

You been addicted for years and you're not sure you have what it takes to ever stop.

You've been overcome by a traumatic event and the pit feels too deep.

You've been dating for what seems like an eternity and you're not sure you'll ever find the one for you.

You've been chronically sick for so long that feeling healthy and stable seems beyond your grasp.

You've run into a dead end with your career and you can't seem to find anything meaningful to do.

What does the ache and longing look like for you? Where do you feel fully surrendered and yet nothing seems to be changing? Do you sometimes want to take off your boots and stop walking altogether? Or do you think you could be dared to take just one more step? Just. One. More.

Do you think the adventure of life change, even with its valleys, could be more compelling than sitting down and not going any farther? Could you consider the journey towards this complete and abundant life to be as meaningful as the final destination? Could you keep going even if you knew there were parts of your life that won't change the way you'd like? Could you do it if you realized that your next step looked a lot like waiting?

These are tricky questions because they touch on some of the most emotional territory of transformation. The sour moments are so much more painful to wrap our hearts around than the sweet ones are, aren't they? Sometimes all we are left with is our questions echoing back to us with silence. "Why God? Why is this happening to me? Why can't this end? Why aren't you doing anything to change it?"

It makes sense to ask these questions of God. After all, we've said throughout this entire book that God is the One who actually brings about our transformation, and he does it because he loves us and wants to make us whole. Sure, we have to open ourselves to vulnerability and surrender our lives to change, but when we've done that and still don't experience the change we long for, is God to blame?

The truth is that there is no guarantee that all the things we want and need to change will actually change on this side of heaven. There is no automatic ticket to transformation just because we are willing or desperate.

Our List of Longings

I have a long list of longings and a heart heavy with things I just want to see changed. I'm tired of waiting. There are days I feel bloated with disappointment because the life change I'm aching for feels like a mirage that's too far in the distance. I keep struggling with the same insecurities I've had for decades. I ask the same questions without getting any answers. I get weary in the waiting. I feel weak and stop dead in my tracks with discouragement. I want to make a permanent home in my sweatpants and give up. I understand impatience and disappointment full well.

But here's what I'm learning: moving towards freedom, from death to rebirth, is very, very rarely instantaneous.

Dallas Willard once said, "The approach to wholeness is for humankind a process of great length and difficulty that engages all our own powers to their fullest extent over a long course of experience." In some matters, complete transformation takes our entire lifetime and sometimes into the next. Scripture tells us that all creation groans, and the groaning will not end until Jesus returns. We groan because we long for light to push back the darkness in ourselves and in our world. I want to be healthier and I want the same for people around me. I want the hurts of our world to be healed once and for all.

The truth is, not everything that's broken will be made new on this side of heaven. But, experiencing abundance in certain parts of your life always leaves you with an urge for more. It's addicting like that.

I love how C.S. Lewis captures it: "If I find in myself a desire which no experience in this world can satisfy, then the most probable explanation is that I was made for another world." So how will you and I live with this yearning, even though we're not really meant to carry it? How do we hold the heaviness of our aches and navigate our list of longings? Will we white-knuckle our way through life, or could we live expectantly with hope and faith that God will one day breathe new life into our most desperate places? Could we actually trust that God knows the exact and perfectly right time to make all things new? Can we walk out our own journeys, even the hard parts, with our eyes fixed on that distant horizon instead of tripping up over ourselves? Let's echo the wise words of author Shauna Niequist: "When life is sweet, say thank you and celebrate. And when life is bitter, say thank you and grow." So let's not give up and stop. Let's keep taking faithful steps forward.

Even Heroes Wait

Great heroes of faith faced the same struggles we do. They were not exempt from those questions that burn deep within. In fact, men and women of deep faith seemed to ask themselves even more questions. The type of questions that faced reality head on. They are the questions that unlock the power to keep going. What will I gain if I keep walking, even though I might not arrive at my destination? Does this journey have meaning in and of itself?

The men and women acclaimed as heroes in Scripture knew something of waiting and longing, and of keeping the long view in mind. Think of Abraham, Jacob, Joseph and Moses, Sarah, Rahab and David, to name just a few. We know, for instance, that "Abraham was first named 'father' and then became a father because he dared to trust God to do what only God could do: raise the dead to life, with a word make something out of nothing. When everything was hopeless, Abraham believed anyway, deciding to live not on the basis of what he saw he couldn't do but on what God said he would do." (Romans 4:17b-18) Abraham had set his faith and hope in his God to restore and redeem. He saw God's hand at work in the minutiae of his life but he still needed to focus on the long view in order to stand firm in faith. His faith was in the hope that one day God's promises would come true, even if it didn't happen in his lifetime.

These heroes lived with longing and are commended for it. None of them experienced what God had promised while they were still alive on earth. Imagine, living a lifetime well aware of your need for God's intervention and yet not seeing it come to pass the way you'd envisioned at any time in your life? They lived and died, yearning for what was broken to be made new, but they lived full of faith, anticipating the day God would completely reform and restore it all. They knew there was more to life than what they could see and that's why they held the long view.

They lived with hope, expecting their longings would one day be no more, but satisfied to thrive where God placed them. They considered themselves aliens and strangers on earth, just passing through to their true home—the perfect place they had been made for. They persevered through the grand transformation of their lives, living expectantly and choosing to hold onto hope for what they saw far off in the distance. These heroes show us the way to frame the "in-the-meantime" moments.

"In the meantime" can be an adventure rather than an exercise in killing time; persevering versus enduring; flourishing instead of simply surviving; dynamic and not static. Author Barbara Kingsolver says, "The very least you can do in your life is to figure out what you hope for. And the most you can do is live inside that hope. Not admire it from a distance but live right in it, under its roof."

What do we hope for? We hope for the day when this off-tune song of longing will end.

What can we have faith for? We can trust one day the groaning will stop and every part will come together in harmony. All of creation will be made perfect and whole. The need for transformation will be no more, and each of us will be standing as the Bride at the altar with her Bridegroom, singing, "Holy, Holy is the Lord

God Almighty who was and is and is to come." That's the hope we can live inside of. That's the symphony we were made for and the song we will sing together. It is the point on the horizon we can fix our eyes on when we are not sure we can take another step.

Let's take encouragement from knowing that there have been many pilgrims who have walked the same path before us. They surround us like a large crowd in a stadium cheering us on to victory. They know that as I fix my gaze on the long view, I will be fixing my gaze on Jesus. He's the Author of my life and he's writing a beautiful story within each of us. He's the Perfecter of our faith; we can be strong and not wither when the way seems too difficult.

Jesus himself kept the long view in mind while he endured the cross and all the shame of death. He was able to endure the pain because he knew it would lead to the greatest joy: the joy of swallowing up death with life. His gaze was fixed on his Father. Pain and brokenness were buried so that healing and wholeness could rise and flourish. It's a mystery to embrace, no doubt, but I can keep the long view and endure the struggle because I also have access to this transforming power.

A Final Word

In a last intimate meal with his closest friends, Jesus told his disciples that he was leaving them. They didn't know what he was talking about, but Jesus knew the life he was daring them to live would require an Encourager, an Advocate and a Counselor—someone who could help navigate the way. He knew they would need him and so he promised them his Spirit as their companion. He called them friends, and he knew they would need one another in order to hold on to the long view.

Those disciples were in their own process of being transformed. They had already been changed as they hung out with Jesus; they had caught glimpses of heaven on earth as they discovered for themselves what an abundant life really was all about. I can only imagine the conversations this tiny band of friends had together with Jesus as they traveled from town to town. But when Jesus left this earth, having conquered death, he commissioned his friends to love. He asked them to spread the word about the kind of life that truly satisfies. He told them to care for the vulnerable and marginalized and to help people conform their lives to a new way—the way of love.

Jesus dares us to do the same. He invites us to join as family, relying on his Spirit to keep the long view and bring the Kingdom "on earth as it is in heaven"—to literally help usher in this abundant life of love. The disciples were filled with the Spirit to do this work and we are too. We're not just living for Jesus, we are living from him. In this way our burden is made light.

As I look back on my life, and in particular the most remarkable transformation of being reborn out of personal tragedy, I know that risking it all and daring myself to surrender to the process of transformation is worth it. I know that leaning into vulnerability—even though it feels like I'm losing the very life that keeps me feeling safe—is the pathway to becoming the best version of myself.

Sometimes my prayers to be changed are more of an obligation than a desire, but deep down I know I really want change. I want to respond to God nudging me out of my comfort zone. I want to trust him in the hard places instead of distracting myself with things that numb the fear. I want to remember that life is not about being perfect but about becoming perfect.

I want to live expectantly, knowing one day everything will be exactly as it should. I want to trust that this adventure is more compelling than sitting down and not taking another step; to consider that the journey toward this complete, whole life is worth all the struggle. I want to walk toward abundance with boldness and confidence because I know the One who has the power to change everything is changing me.

God isn't transforming me to be more perfect so he can love me more—he's transforming me so I can experience his love more perfectly.

I want to keep going. And I want you to keep going too, brave pilgrim. Here's a promise for us to cling to.

God, like no other, transforms cold, dark places and makes them beautiful.

He mends the broken and refreshes the weary.

He restores the smoldering and dying and gives hope for new life.

He really does make all things new. And he's promised to make you and me new too.

Ultreïa! Ultreïa! Ultreïa!

"I'm not saying that I have this all together, that I have it made. But I am well on my way, reaching out for Christ, who has so wondrously reached out for me.

Friends, don't get me wrong: By no means do I count myself an expert in all of this, but I've got my eye on the goal, where God is beckoning us onward—to Jesus. I'm off and running, and I'm not turning back."

— Philippians 3:12-14

AFTERWORD

Everyone wants to be loved by someone, right?

I think we all want to love someone too.

Buying that perfect gift to show a special someone how much he or she is loved is a thrill. Planning a surprise, bringing flowers, or cooking someone's favorite meal are things that make us feel good. Is there anything more fulfilling than showing someone how much we care?

Yes, we love to love.

We've learned through the entire book that being transformed by God is the way to be freed up to experience his love in extraordinary ways. We've been loved first by God in order that we may experience more love. Love begets more love.

I'd hate to miss this opportunity to band together as a collective to embrace life's dare and make a real impact. There are many people on the planet who are unsung heroes of courage and faith but are in need of tangible resources to make a way forward. They need our love in real-time. The world I imagine in my dreams is when big, bold love reigns!

That's why I'm inviting you to love.

I've had the great honor of becoming friends with community leaders in different parts of the world. I've sat in their homes, in their schools and in their offices talking about the real challenges they are working to address—particularly the needs of vulnerable girls. Whether it's the challenge of breaking a cycle of abuse and slavery, the opportunity to be educated or reducing the rates of early marriage, these leaders know what they are doing—and have great ideas of how to meet these challenges—but need partners to join them.

Don't we all need a partner? Don't we all need someone else's love to help and heal and change us for the better? Partnership isn't weakness. It's relationship. And we know that God uses relationships to transform it all.

"Love drives out all fear. Love conquers all." (1 John 4:18) What if this wasn't just a quotable sentiment, but a promise? Could our tangible love remove the tangible fear from one little girl's heart? Could our tangible love overcome tangible barriers for those community leaders trying to rescue and provide a way for the most vulnerable? I don't think it does, I *know* it does. I've seen it with my own eyes and felt it in my own heart.

If you have been moved by any part of this book; if any of the words helped you, then please see that as God's tangible way of loving you.

Now it's time to turn that love into more love.

I'm daring you to show your love in tangible ways by being a part of the ***Love2Love Project.***

Let's love together!

Visit **LifesGreatDare.com** to learn more about how you can get involved.

LOVE2LOVE

PROJECT

Thank you!

Reflection Guide

Here are a few questions to help you process the ideas and thoughts that have come to mind while you are reading. I'd suggest looking at them after you have finished each chapter and returning to them again after you have finished the whole book. Better yet, find a trusted friend or a small group who will read the book with you so you can reflect on the questions together.

Part I- Embracing the Dare

Chapter One: The Haircut That Changed My Life

1. When in your life have you taken a step of courage (big or small) and risked something? Why did you do it? How did it feel? What happened?

2. *"What if transformation wasn't about God making me more perfect so he could love me more, but instead was about changing me so I could experience his love more perfectly?"* Have you ever considered why God wants to transform you? How does it make you feel to know that our transformation is motivated by God's love for us and always leads to more love?

3. What do you want to be transformed in your life? Try to get as specific as possible.

4. If God is as central to the process as this chapter explains, what do you think your next step should be in relating to God as you read this book?

Chapter Two: Yes Changes Everything

1. Christa talks about the two big questions she had for God. What questions do you have for God?

2. How do you experience God loving you? Can you recall a specific event or moment when you felt secure in how much you were loved?

3. The rich, full, abundant life always includes more peace and joy and love. In what ways have you experienced this "abundance" in your own life? What do you think is getting in the way of experiencing more and more of this in a deeper way? What are some practical steps you could take to begin experiencing life more abundantly?

Part II- Transform Me

Chapter Three: From Bud to Bloom

1. *"Transformation is a process, but it's not a formula."* As you look at the eight themes of transformation, what intrigues you the most? Does anything surprise you about the process?

2. As you consider accepting life's great dare to let God transform you, what excites you the most about this journey? What concerns you? Any other thoughts or emotions worth noting?

Chapter Four: Open

1. What is an area of your life where you feel broken or stuck?

2. What might that area look like if it were mended and made whole?

3. Where do you need to be gentle with yourself in this process? Do you have any self-talk that is sabotaging your transformation?

Chapter Five: Surrender

1. What are some things that you cling to in order to feel secure, satisfied and significant, but that are actually getting in the way of you becoming the best version of yourself?

2. How does it feel to consider loosening your grasp and surrendering them?

3. What is one thing that strikes you about the story of Peter walking on the water? How does this apply to your own journey of stepping into transformation?

Chapter Six: Vulnerability

1. Where have you felt vulnerable in the past? Be specific. What does it feel like?

2. When has feeling vulnerable gotten in your way of making a choice and growing into a better version of yourself? If you were faced with the same choice again, what could you do differently?

3. How does it make you feel knowing Jesus faced the same vulnerability you experience?

4. In what ways could vulnerability actually be a good thing in your own process of transformation?

5. What's making you feel vulnerable these days?

Chapter Seven: Death

1. *"Some things must die to make room for something new."* How have you experienced this in your life?

2. The key to change is identifying the habit, attitude or approach to life that is holding us back from a more abundant life. It's the thing that needs to "die". What is this for you? What needs to die?

3. What is difficult about having this part of you "die"? What do you need to help you stay "in the death zone" of transformation while something new is being born?

Chapter Eight: Starless Night. Morning Light.

1. Christa shares her personal story to illustrate her own dramatic transformation and experience in "the death zone". What is one thing you've learned about transformation from her story?

2. Is there anything from your own story that would be an encouragement to someone else? What can you do to share it with someone?

Chapter Nine: Rebirth

1. As you look back on your own life, where have you seen new life (in your habits, attitudes, approaches) emerge from old ones? What have you learned about "rebirth" that can be applied to your present-day transformation process?

2. What threatens to push you off the path of the new habit, attitude or approach that is being formed in you? What do you need to stay on this path?

3. How are you relating to God as a "coach"? Is he a tyrant or a caring mentor-figure guiding your way? What difference would it make in your journey of transformation if you were to relate to God as a coach who encourages and guides you?

Chapter Ten: Freedom

1. How do you feel about the idea that the perfect freedom we crave actually comes when we are radically dependent on God? What makes you feel that way? How do you think this impacts your own journey of transformation?

2. In what area of your life do you feel you're being invited to put your full weight down on God? What about this makes you most afraid or anxious?

3. What are the practical things that are holding you back from stepping out into the freedom you're being invited into?

Chapter Eleven: Love

1. *"We are freed up from our old ways so that we can love better."* If you were to love yourself better, what could that look like? If you were to love God better, what could that look like? If you were to love others better, what could that look like?

2. When you think about the areas in your life where you've experienced transformation, how has that made the world a better place?

3. What do you think might be at stake if you don't submit to the transformation that's currently needed in your life? What "love" will be locked up tight and not given away?

4. Go back to the five questions at the end of the chapter and take some time to answer each one. Don't rush through them, rather, get super-practical with them and create an action plan for each.

Part III- Ultreïa!

Chapter Twelve: Keep Going!
1. Have you ever had a difficult situation where you had to dig deep and do something you didn't think you were capable of doing? How might that situation help you as you "keep going" in your own transformation?

2. What part of your own transformation is making you weary these days? What type of encouragement do you need?

3. What encouragement, if any, do you get from knowing that the effort to "keep going" will pay off?

Chapter Thirteen: Seek the Sweet
1. What "sweet" moments in your life have changed you? Be specific about both the moments and how they have changed you. Take a moment and thank God for these moments.

2. What are some of the things that get in your way of "taking notice" and living on a regular basis with gratitude and reverence? What could you do differently to see and savor God more in the ordinary, everyday sweet moments? Be specific about the ideas and make a plan to try them out.

Chapter Fourteen: We're in This Together
1. *"He uses family, friends, and sometimes strangers in every*

aspect of our transformation." How have you seen this manifest in your own life?

2. Have you invited anyone else into your life to support you on your transformation journey? If you have, are they reading this book with you? If you haven't found someone, what could be your next step in identifying someone to join you?

3. How are you making yourself available to companion others on their personal transformation journeys? Who comes to mind and how can you make it known to them that you're available?

Chapter Fifteen: Hold the Long View

1. Is there an area in your life where you genuinely feel desperate to see transformation but it seems like it will never come? How does this make you feel? Why do you think it's important to identify this?

2. How does it feel to know there were many people called "heroes" in Scripture who never experienced what they were longing for?

3. The role of faith, trust and hope seems to be important to this "in-between" time. Is there anything you can do to grow your faith, trust and hope in God during this time?

For a free PDF of these reflections and other free resources
visit **LifesGreatDare.com**

ACKNOWLEDGMENTS

It took me two and a half years to read *Charlotte's Web* as a kid. That's my first memory of not really being interested in books. It wasn't that I couldn't read well, I just preferred running around and playing outside to curling up with a book. And that became the internal script for me for most of my life, which is why I never ever aspired to write a book. I think this is why the "Acknowledgments" section means so much to me.

One of my favorite musicians is *Sleeping At Last*. I have a secret wish that Ryan would create a soundtrack to the story of my life! In one of his more recent songs he says, "through this magnifying glass I see a thousand finger prints on the surfaces of who I am." (Atlas: Son, 2015). There are so many people who have influenced me, encouraged me and are a part of my story. I can trace the lines of their imprints into the details of this project. I can see them, each a thread that has been woven into the fabric of who I am.

There are too many people to name here, and yet I'm so very grateful for you all.

Teachers, neighbors, pastors and youth leaders, mentors, professors, roommates and past employers, authors, therapists, musicians, church communities and friends who have become family through the seasons of my life. I am a blessed woman!

This book has been a labor of love with many, many "midwives" helping to birth it.

For Tim — your nudging me to write was the permission I needed to give myself and explore the new thing God wanted to do in me. I'm eternally grateful.

For early readings and feedback, thank you to Joel, Rick, Tim, Lindsay, Ben and Natalie. You have no idea just how valuable your expertise and encouragement were for me to keep going and to keep getting better.

For the generosity of these families as they gave me a quiet space to get away and write: Otts, Emmons, Bartletts and Millers — thank you!

For Ally and Darrell Vesterfelt and the Author Launch community — it took me about six months to come to grips with even calling myself an "author", but your support and friendship throughout the process was exactly what I needed.

For Dave Fretz and Diego Lopez — it was a joy working with you on the layout and design of this book — you're both pros!

For Susan Fish, Kathryn Smithyman and Rebecca Sjonger — thank you for helping make the manuscript much better with your expert editing. You made this first-timer love the process!

I know I could go on. Over these past three years there have been so many hallway conversations, check-ins and affirmations by colleagues, friends and family. Don't underestimate for a moment how significant your part was in making this book a reality.

Dad and Mom — there are not enough "good words" in me to tell you and the world how much you mean to me. I love you very much. Honest in our house.

Notes

Introduction

p. 1   Søren Kierkegaard (1813–1855) was a Danish writer and philosopher.

PART I- Embracing the Dare

p. 5   "Dare: to have the boldness to try; venture; hazard..." http://dictionary.reference.com/browse/dare, accessed on June 23, 2015.

Chapter One: The Haircut That Changed My Life

p. 7   "...and then the day came when the risk..." This quotation is widely attributed to author and journal writer Anaïs Nin (1903–1977), however there is some dispute as to its authorship.

p. 14   *Holy Bible, New Living Translation* (Wheaton: Tyndale House Publishers, Inc, 1996) Matthew 13:44-46.

p. 17   "I don't know Who—or What—put the question..." Dag Hammarskjöld was a Swedish diplomat, the second United Nations Secretary-General, and a Nobel Peace Prize recipient. He is the author of *Markings* (London: Faber and Faber, 1964).

p. 19   "We do not just drift into becoming the best version of ourselves." John Ortberg, *The Me I Want to Be, Teen Edition: Becoming God's Best Version of You* (Grand Rapids: Zondervan, 2010) 20.

Chapter Two: Yes Changes Everything

p. 21   "How glorious the splendor..." This quote is attributed to Brennan Manning (1934-2013), a Franciscan monk and author of popular books such as *The Ragamuffin Gospel* (which is quoted later in the book), *The Signature of Jesus* and *Ruthless Trust.*

p. 24   "They decided to eat from the tree of 'I know what's best'." This whole idea is not my own, but rather something I heard many times from a teaching pastor at a great church I was a part of for over twelve years. Bruxy Cavey is the author of *The End of Religion* and leads at The Meeting House Church in Ontario, Canada. Find him at **www.bruxy.com**

p. 25   "Ever since the snake said..." Henri Nouwen, *In the Name of Jesus: Reflections on Christian Leadership* (New York: The Crossroads Publishing Company, 1989) 77.

p. 26   "It's what Love Does..." Bob Goff, *Love Does: Discover a Secretly Incredible Life in an Ordinary World* (Nashville: Thomas Nelson, 2012).

p. 29   "To me, the whole universe is this giant, breathing hymn." Michael Gungor, via @michaelgungor on Twitter, February 4, 2015. Michael Gungor is the leader of the Grammy-nominated musical collective, Gungor.

p. 29   "Finally, brothers and sisters, whatever is true, whatever is noble, whatever is right, whatever is pure, whatever is lovely, whatever is admirable—if anything is excellent or praiseworthy— think about such things." *Holy Bible, New International Version* (Colorado Springs: Biblica, 2011) Philippians 4:8.

p. 30   "The secret of the mystery is..." Brennan Manning, *The Ragamuffin Gospel* (Colorado Springs: Multnomah Books, 2005) 207.

PART II- Transform Me

Chapter Three: From Bud to Bloom

p. 33   "Transform: to change in form..."
http://dictionary.reference.com/browse/transform
accessed on June 23, 2015.

p. 35   "No, it is not yours to open buds into blossoms..." Sir Rabindranath Tagore, *Fruit-Gathering XVIII* (New York: The MacMillan Company, 1916) http://www.eldritchpress.org/rt/fg.htm, accessed on August 4, 2015.

Chapter Four: Open

p. 41   "He who is outside his door has the hardest part of his journey behind him." Dutch Proverb (hey, I had to pay homage to my Dutch roots!)

p. 47   There are a few places in the Bible that describe Jesus inviting the disciples to follow him: Matthew 4:18–22, Mark 1:16–20, Luke 5:1–11 and John 1:35–51.

Chapter Five: Surrender

p. 51   "We must be willing to let go of the life..." This quote has been attributed both to American writer and philosopher Joseph Campbell (1904-1987) and to English novelist E. M. Forster (1879–1970).

p. 55   "Once a character is in disharmony..." Donald Miller, *Storyline 2.0* (Nashville: Storyline Design, 2012) 69.

p. 56   This story of Peter walking on the water is found in the Bible, Matthew 14:22-34. I'd suggest reading the story before it about Jesus feeding the crowd. Reading it in a few different translations (e.g., NIV, New Living, The Message) can be helpful.

Chapter Six: Vulnerability

p. 61   "Have the courage to be imperfect..." Dr. Brené Brown, Excerpts from TEDTalk: The Power of Vulnerability, 2010. https://www.ted.com/talks/brene_brown_on_vulnerability?language=en Dr. Brené Brown, Ph.D., is a research professor at the University of Houston Graduate College of Social Work. She studies vulnerability, courage, worthiness and shame.

p. 62   "Risk" by William Arthur Ward (1921-1994), American writer and poet. Cited in *A Pilgrim's Guide to the Camino de Santiago* by John Brierley (Camino Guides, 2013).

p. 64   "I learned that courage was not the absence of fear..." This quote is attributed to Nelson Mandela (1918–2013), a South African anti-apartheid revolutionary, politician and philanthropist who served as President of South Africa from 1994 to 1999.

p. 65   "Fear keeps a life small." Ann Voskamp, *One Thousand Gifts* (Grand Rapids: Zondervan, 2010) 145.

p. 68   This story of Jesus being tempted by Satan for forty days in the wilderness is found in the Bible in Matthew 4:1-11.

Chapter Seven: Death

p. 71   "Living aware of your soul's deep longings..." Jonathan Martin via @theboyonthebike on Twitter, February 5, 2015. Jonathan Martin is teaching pastor at Sanctuary Church in Tulsa, OK.

p. 72   "Our route to psychological wholeness..." Will Hernandez, *Henri Nouwen and Spiritual Polarities: A Life of Tension* (New York: Paulist Press) 6.

p. 73   "The whole spiritual life is learning how to die..." Eugene Peterson interviewed by Mark Galli (March 4, 2005) "Spirituality for All the Wrong Reasons". *Christianity Today*, 49(3), 42. http://www.christianitytoday.com/ct/2005/march/26.42.html

p. 73   The story of Moses leading the Israelites out of the Egypt can be found in the Bible in the book of Exodus.

p. 74   "In order to free the captive, one must name the captivity." Brennan Manning, *The Ragamuffin Gospel* (Colorado Springs: Multnomah Books, 2005) 134.

p. 78   Viktor Frankl chronicles his experience as a prisoner in a Nazi concentration camp in his book *Man's Search for Meaning* (Boston: Beacon Press, 2006).

p. 78   "Suffering is the midwife to maturity." Chris Heuertz, @ ChrisHeuertz via Twitter, February 15, 2014.

p. 79   "Jesus' big message [is] that there is something essential..." Richard Rohr, adapted from *Dying: We Need It for Life* and *The Spirituality of Imperfection* available through Franciscan Media, http://catalog.franciscanmedia.org

p. 79   *Holy Bible, New Living Translation* 2 Corinthians 4:10.

p. 80   *Holy Bible, New Living Translation* Philippians 3:7, 8, 10, 11.

Chapter Eight: Starless Night. Morning Light.

p. 81   "Then their shining stopped..." Poem by Ann Weems, "Lament Psalm #27" *Psalms of Lament* (Louisville: Westminster John Knox Press, 1995) 53.

p. 86   Ibid.

p. 89   "Those who believe in God—but without passion in the heart..." Miguel de Unamuno y Jugo, *Tragic Sense of Life* (1912) *213*. He was a nineteenth century Spanish philosopher and novelist.

p. 91   "New life always starts in the dark." Barbara Brown Taylor, *Learning to Walk in the Dark* (New York: Harper Collins Publishers, 2014) 129.

Chapter Nine: Rebirth

p. 93   "The lotus flower blooms most beautifully from the deepest and thickest mud." Ancient Buddhist Proverb.

p. 96   There are many resources online that describe the process of metamorphosis. I found this video particularly helpful: https://www.youtube.com/watch?v=7AUeM8MbaIk, accessed on April 24, 2013.

p. 99   "I was saved...I am being saved...I will be saved..." This nugget of wisdom was shared with me by my friend Tim Day. He's the author of *God Enters Stage Left*. You should check him out at **www.timday.org**

p. 99   "Spiritual transformation is not behavior modification..." This idea is taken from an incredibly valuable resource by Dallas Willard and John Ortberg, *Living in Christ's Presence: Final Words on Heaven and the Kingdom of God*. I accessed it through audio book format by Christian Audio, 2013. http://christianaudio.com/living-in-christs-presence-dallas-willard-john-ortberg-audiobook-download. It is also available in DVD and hardcover book on Amazon.

p. 103   "Jesus said, 'Live ecstatically. Move out of that place of death and toward life...'" Henri Nouwen, *"Intimacy, Fecundity, Ecstasy"* (*Radix*, May/June 1984) 23.

Chapter Ten: Freedom

p. 105 "Tomorrow's freedom is today's surrender." All Sons & Daughters from song *Dawn to Dusk*. Take a listen here: https://www.youtube.com/watch?v=Jb5zQv9kXW4

p. 106 These examples of how Jesus provided physical freedom for people can be found in the Bible: healing group of lepers (Luke 17:11-19); healing a woman from blood disease (Luke 8:43-48); healing a paralyzed man brought to Jesus by his friends (Luke 5:17-26).

p. 107 Story of Mary being restored is found in John 8:1-11, Zacchaeus (Luke 19:1-10), Peter (Luke 22:54-62, John 21:15-17), Paul (Acts 9:1-31).

p. 108 The image of the wedding feast portrayed in Scripture is found in Matthew 22:1-14, Luke 14:15, and Revelation 19:7-9.

p. 113 *The Fault in Our Stars* by John Green. Movie directed by Josh Boone, 2014. Watch the clip here: https://www.youtube.com/watch?v=9rB3e8-6PUw

Chapter Eleven: Love

p. 115 "If sympathy for the world's wounds is not enlarged..." Nicholas Wolterstorff, *Lament for a Son* (Grand Rapids: Wm. B. Eerdmans Publishing Co., 1987). 92, 93.

p. 118 "To the degree that we are transformed, the world is transformed." Phileena Heuertz. *The Work of the People* https://www.facebook.com/theworkofthepeople/posts/10152027899590682?__fns&hash=Ac28GWhoymIYZHKp

p. 121 "We are put on earth for a little space...". "The Little Black Boy" by William Blake, *Songs of Innocence and Experience*

(London, 1789/1784).

p. 122 "We are a transforming community that transforms communities..." This was a statement used to guide The Meeting House Church during their TRANSFORM Mission. **www.themeetinghouse.com**

p. 122 "As you love deeply, the ground of your heart..." Henri Nouwen, *The Inner Voice of Love: A Journey Through Anguish to Freedom* (New York: Doubleday, 1996) 59.

p. 124 "The Apostle Paul spends a great deal of time addressing transformation...." I am specifically referring to his second letter to the Corinthian Church. 2 Corinthians 3–5.

p. 126 "I imagine God sees who I'll become as I start RSVPing 'yes'..." Bob Goff, *Love Does: Discover a Secretly Incredible Life in an Ordinary World* (Nashville: Thomas Nelson, 2012) 130.

PART III- Ultreïa!

p. 129 "The word "Ultreïa" has the meaning of "onward", or "keep going"..." http://www.hymnology.co.uk/u/ultreia, accessed June 23, 2015.

Chapter Twelve: Keep Going!

p. 131 "The mystery of human existence..." Fyodor Dostoyevsky, *The Brothers Karamazov* (Russia, 1880).

Chapter Thirteen: Seek the Sweet

p. 135 "For the grateful person knows that God is good..." Thomas Merton, *Thoughts in Solitude* (New York: Farrar, Straus, Giroux, 1956) 43.

p.137   "God will bring people and events into our lives..." Thomas Keating, *The Heart of the World: An introduction to contemplative Christianity* (New York: The Crossroads Publishing Company, 2008) 41.

p. 138   "The exercise of reverence generally includes knowing your rank..." Barbara Brown Taylor, *An Altar in the World: A Geography of Faith* (New York: HarperOne, 2009) 19.

p. 139   "As long as you're a spectator in your life..." Allison Vesterfelt, *Packing Light: Thoughts on Living Life with Less Baggage* (Chicago: Moody Publishers, 2013) 221. I should also note that Allison and her husband Darrell have been incredibly helpful in bringing this book to fruition. They have an amazing online course called Author Launch. Check it out: **www.authorlaunch.com**

Chapter Fourteen: We're In This Together

p. 141   "Kinship is a rich bondedness that calls forth to the deepest parts..." Joyce Rupp, *Praying our Goodbyes* (Notre Dame: Ave Maria Press, 1988) 109.

p. 146   "There can be no vulnerability without risk..." M. Scott Peck, *The Different Drum: Community Making and Peace* (New York: Touchstone, 1987) 233.

Chapter Fifteen: Hold the Long View

p. 147   "Waiting time is not wasting time..." Henri Nouwen via @HenriNouwen on Twitter, March 19, 2014.

p. 147   "Apparently it takes the average Camino pilgrim..." This information was taken from a book I read as I prepared for the Camino. It was by Kurt Koontz called, *A Million Steps,* 2013.

p. 149 "Waiting...it means struggling with the vision of who we really are..." Sue Monk Kidd, *When the Heart Waits: Spiritual Direction for Life's Sacred Questions* (San Francisco: Harper & Row, 1990) 14.

p. 152 "The approach to wholeness is for humankind a process..." Dallas Willard, *The Spirit of the Disciplines: Understanding How God Changes Lives* (New York: Harper Collins, 1988) 70.

p. 152 "If I find in myself a desire which no experience in this world..." C.S. Lewis, *Mere Christianity* (San Francisco: Harper Collins, 2001) 136.

p. 153 "When life is sweet, say thank you and celebrate..." Shauna Niequist, *Bittersweet: Thoughts on Change, Grace, and Learning the Hard Way* (Grand Rapids: Zondervan, 2010) 13.

p. 153 "The men and women acclaimed as heroes in Scripture". Of course, you can learn more of their individual stories in the Old Testament, but take some time to read Hebrews 11:1–12:3 to amplify your reading of this section of the book.

p. 153 "Abraham was first named 'father' and then *became* a father..." Eugene H. Peterson. *The Message: The Bible in Contemporary Language* (Colorado Springs: NavPress) 2002. Romans 4:17b-18.

p. 154 "The very least you can do in your life..." Barbara Kingsolver, *Animal Dreams: A Novel* (New York: Harper Perennial, 1990).

p. 154 "Holy, holy, holy is the Lord God Almighty..." This reference is found in a few places in Scripture (Isaiah 6:3 & Revelation 4:8).

p. 155 "Jesus knew the life he was daring them to live would require an Encourager, an Advocate and a Counselor..." I highly recommend reading John 13-17 sometime. A full reading through these five chapters is one of my favorite ways to get back to the essence of Jesus' message. This was the last recorded conversation he had with his best friends before he was killed.

p. 156 "We're not just living *for* Jesus we are living *from* him." The truth is, I did not come up with this on my own, but I'm not entirely sure where I picked it up. I have an inkling it may be from a great author, Emily Freeman. If not, I'm happy to give her the credit! She's published a few great books I've read: *Grace for the Good Girl: Letting Go of the Try-Hard Life* (2012) and *A Million Little Ways: Uncover the Art You were Made to Live* (2013). You can find her online at **www.emilypfreeman.com**

p. 157 *The Message* Philippians 3:12-14.